Stress Relief for Teachers

D0225163

Are you a dedicated teacher wondering why you do not enjoy your job any more?

Do you worry about the students you teach and how you can help them?

Have you found the stress you and your students work under is becoming increasingly unbearable?

This book explains the nature of stress in the classroom in a clear, practical way, focusing on how teachers can help themselves cope, and in turn, help the students in their care.

The author, an experienced clinical psychologist, educational psychologist, researcher and lecturer, introduces the 'Coping Triangle', which is a coping framework based on the principles of cognitive-behavioural therapy. She shows how using this easy-to-implement framework in everyday life can make a positive difference to teachers' lives and will equip them to tackle some of the key challenges they often face in themselves as well as their students such as:

- Stress
- Anger
- Depression
- Anxiety
- Bereavement
- Chronic illness
- Abuse

Not only can the use of the 'Coping Triangle' help people cope with their existing difficulties, it can also be used to prevent these difficulties developing into much more serious issues, such as depression and anxiety. Free of jargon and full of case studies and exercises, this book will be a breath of fresh air to the most jaded of classroom teachers, and will be equally valuable to students on initial teacher education courses.

Dr Claire Hayes has worked as a teacher in mainstream and special education and a Children's Hospital. She has also worked as a clinical psychologist in a wide range of settings including Children's Hospitals, a Child Sexual Abuse Assessment Unit, and an Early Services Intervention Service. She worked for seven years as lecturer in the Education Department in the National University of Ireland Maynooth and has researched areas such as stress, bereavement, and chronic illness as well as prevention of depression and anxiety. She currently works in private practice and has a particular interest in teaching psychological principles as a means of prevention.

Stress Relief for Teachers
The 'Coping Triangle'

Claire Hayes

Routledge
Taylor & Francis Group

LONDON AND NEW YORK

First published 2006 by Routledge
2 Park Square, Milton Park, Abingdon, Oxon OX14 4RN

Simultaneously published in the USA and Canada
by Routledge
270 Madison Avenue, New York, NY 10016

Routledge is an imprint of the Taylor & Francis Group

© 2006 Claire Hayes

Typeset in Sabon by Keyword Group
Printed and bound in Great Britain by TJ International Ltd, Padstow,
Cornwall

All rights reserved. No part of this book may be reprinted or
reproduced or utilised in any form or by any electronic, mechanical,
or other means, now known or hereafter invented, including
photocopying and recording, or in any information storage or retrieval
system, without permission in writing from the publishers.

British Library Cataloguing in Publication Data
A catalogue record for this book is available from the British Library

Library of Congress Cataloging in Publication Data
A catalog record has been requested for this book

ISBN10: 0-415-36933-9 (hbk)
ISBN10: 0-415-36934-7 (pbk)

ISBN13: 9-78-0-415-36933-6 (hbk)
ISBN13: 9-78-0-415-36934-3 (pbk)

For my parents
Joy and Liam

Oh, the comfort, the inexpressible comfort of feeling safe with a person;
Having neither to weigh thoughts nor measure words,
But to pour them all out, just as they are, chaff and grain together,
Knowing that a faithful hand will take and sift them,
Keep what is worth keeping,
And then, with the breath of kindness,
Blow the rest away.

George Eliot (1819–1880)

Contents

Acknowledgements

I am grateful to everyone who has helped me on my journey to writing this book. It started almost twenty years ago when my parents and my late aunt and friend, Noreen Barrett, encouraged me in my notion to study psychology to help me be a better teacher.

Dr Oliver Delaney was the Director of my first psychology course and later supervised my first thesis. Thérèse Brady was the Director of my clinical psychology training and encouraged my interests in helping children cope with death through education. They are both now deceased but, like all great teachers, their lessons live on.

The theoretical framework of my clinical training was cognitive-behavioural and while I am grateful to all my clinical supervisors, I am particularly indebted to Dr Tony Bates for recognising and valuing the 'teacher' in me.

My experience working with Professor Patricia Casey as part of the ODIN European programme in preventing depression convinced me of the value of teaching psychological principles as a means of prevention.

Professor Philip Kendall is due a special 'thank you' for his ongoing support and interest as well as for his generosity and trust in allowing me to link in with his work on preventing depression in adolescents using a school-based programme. This was only possible with the aid of adolescents, parents, guidance counsellors and principals who worked with me on the 'Helping Adolescents Cope' research, which was supported financially by the Irish Department of Education and Science. Thank you.

Along the way I have continued to learn more than I ever taught. This was particularly true in the Children's Hospital, Temple Street, and in the Education Department, the National University of Ireland Maynooth. Professor John Coolahan has been a key supporter of the importance of teacher education and his recognition and support of my work has meant a huge amount.

Over ten years ago Dr Kedar Dwivedi and I discovered that we shared a strong commitment to prevention work. I am very grateful to him for his encouragement and advice as I tiptoe into a new world of writing.

And now to my greatest ally, mentor and friend on this journey: Dr Mark Morgan. He has long been respected as an expert on prevention work and I was delighted when he agreed to act as my Supervisor on my Ph.D. in 1998. The best way I can describe his enormous support to me personally and professionally is to compare him to someone turning on powerful floodlights in a football stadium so that a beginner can kick a ball into open goals and then hear loud applause as if the stadium is full.

Dr Morgan, Head of Education in St Patrick's Teacher Training College, is 'Stress Relief for Teachers', and I am honoured that he has written the Foreword for this book.

I would especially like to thank:

- 'Jenny' – my 'star coper' – and her parents, Peter's parents and 'Robert' for allowing me to tell their stories.
- Anne O'Shea for her beautiful artwork.
- All those in Routledge and Keyword who worked on publishing this book for their kind, professional and good humoured approach.
- The children, parents, teachers and guidance counsellors I have been privileged to work with.
- My friends – you know who you are but you probably have no idea of just how much I value your friendship. Please read George Eliot's quote!

Finally, I would like to thank my family – my first and best teachers – and the ones I love the most!

Foreword

To be asked to write a foreword for any important work on stress is a privilege; to do so for a book written by Dr Claire Hayes is an honour. 'Stress' is used in a variety of senses both in the literature and in everyday life. On some points there is agreement. There is a consensus that some level of stress is inevitable in life. In fact it is likely that a degree of stress can enhance performance and even quality of life. There is also agreement that it is not the duration and level of stress that matters as much as the approach that one brings to it.

The point of departure for Claire's work is the cognitive-behavioural model of human functioning and her work is structured around the principal features of that model relating to emotions, cognitions and behaviour. The value of the cognitive-behavioural position is that it does not focus exclusively on one of these but is concerned above all with their interaction.

One of the strong points in this work is the use of the 'Coping Triangle' as a common framework to understand a variety of problems. Having set out her understanding of stress and a model of coping with the effects of stress, Claire goes on to address a number of specific areas that are very often not seen as connected. Anxiety, anger and depression are often treated separately from each other and without a framework that demonstrates how they can be understood in relation to stressful events. Claire's analysis shows how they can be understood and addressed.

A second and related strength stems from Claire's conviction that cognitive-behavioural principles can be understood relatively easily when they are properly explained and placed in a context that people are familiar with. No one is suggesting for a moment that a quick reading of any book is enough to enable teachers to get the control over their lives that they have yearned for. However, what is possible is to give people an insight and a possible re-interpretation of patterns of behaviour that they thought were inevitable. The problem with some thought processes is that they have a way of seeming to reflect how the world is rather than cognitions that construct the way a person perceives the world. An insight that results in questioning the model of our own decision making and thinking can have profound and liberating effects.

Another important feature of Claire's book is in her authentic analysis of the examples that she gives. Never does she resort to patronising over-simplification – a feature that is often found in 'self-help' books. Rather she grounds her explanations in the complex interaction of environment-mind-behaviour, while at the same time, showing how our habits of thinking and behaving frequently lead us into inappropriate forms of behaviour and interactions.

There are very few people who have the experience and expertise to bring to bear on these issues as Claire Hayes. Before going into psychology she worked as a teacher in mainstream, special education and a Children's Hospital. Having studied psychology (both general and clinical psychology), she subsequently worked with children who had experienced the trauma of sexual abuse and children who had chronic illness. Later she worked in teacher education and, during this time, embarked on her Doctoral research. This work featured the use of a psychoeducational programme to help adolescents cope with stress. This programme was implemented by school guidance counsellors and had significantly positive results. In recent times Claire has continued to develop her clinical practice, specialising in the treatment of anxiety conditions, and her examples in her book bear the signs of her experience.

The final point I will make has to do with how Claire's own personality comes through in her writing. Her optimism, her warm personality and her caring attitude are evident in every chapter.

Dr Mark Morgan
Head of Education, St Patrick's College, Dublin
June 2005

1 Introduction

Is the teacher's key role to *teach* students or to *help* students *learn*? The answer is not simple and depends as much on the ability and motivation of the teacher to teach as it does on the ability and motivation of the student to learn. Ability and motivation are in turn dependent on interest and health. Many books have been written for teachers focusing on how to teach, or on how to help students learn. This book is different. Its focus is on helping teachers cope with their role, regardless of how they define it. Teaching can be wonderful – but it can also be very stressful. Good teaching contains multiple rewards for the teacher and student alike. In a positive, energetic learning environment the teacher learns from the student just as the student learns from the teacher. The rewards can be very satisfying – generating enthusiasm, a sense of purpose and excitement. The converse is also true. Wonderful, kind, generous people can begin to hate aspects of their own selves that they see as being 'self-righteous', 'sarcastic' or even 'deliberately malicious and cruel'. Somehow the label 'stressed' can add to the difficulties and can even become the ultimate failure.

This book is different in that its focus is psychoeducational and preventative. It acknowledges that teaching is stressful, but that this is not as important as the perception of the stress and the meaning of the label. The book is aimed at giving people who choose to be teachers tools they can use to develop their own coping resources so that they can continue to do their job to the best of their abilities while at the same time maximising their own sense of job satisfaction and well-being. They, as well as their students, will benefit as a result.

The book is structured around the key cognitive-behavioural principles of emotion, cognition and behaviour. It focuses first on what the 'Coping Triangle' is and how it can be applied to teachers to help them relieve stress in general as well as stress generated from their reactions to their students. Chapters 4, 5, 6 and 7 focus on how teachers can understand their feelings of anger, anxiety and depression and how they can use the 'Coping Triangle' to help cope with these. The 'Coping Triangle' is my way of presenting cognitive-behavioural principles in a preventative way. These principles are not new, however, as is clear from the overview of some of the literature in this area contained in Chapter 8: Theory behind the 'Coping Triangle'. The book concludes by demonstrating how the 'Coping Triangle' can be used to relieve practical stress generated by three different situations: a student telling her teacher that she has been abused, teaching a child who has recently been diagnosed with a severe illness, and finally a stressor most of us have encountered in our teaching careers: teaching students who just do not want to learn!

The predominant model throughout the book is cognitive-behavioural. This is adapted from cognitive-behavioural therapy, originally devised by Dr Aaron Beck. It is now one of the most popular and effective psychological treatments worldwide for treating a wide range of difficulties, such as depression, anxiety, substance abuse, eating disorders and abuse. Its core principles may seem at first glance to be obvious and simplistic: 1 how we *feel* affects how we *think* and what we *do*; 2 how we *think* affects how we *feel* and what we *do*; and 3 what we *do* affects how we *feel* and how we *think*. Obvious and simplistic they may be, but these principles work. In an age of cynicism, burn-out and increasing dissatisfaction, it is time for teachers and students to learn the core cognitive-behavioural principles, to examine and take responsibility for their own ways of feeling, thinking and behaving, as well as their own underlying beliefs, so as to improve the quality of life, decrease the ill effects of stress, and ultimately to prevent serious physical and/or emotional difficulties.

This book has evolved from practice, as well as theory. I am passionate about teaching psychological principles to children, parents, teachers, doctors, nurses, indeed everyone, as a means of helping people cope with their current difficulties and ultimately preventing more serious ones in the future. As a newly trained primary school teacher in 1986 I quickly realised that 'learning by doing' does not work if the student is too crippled with anxiety to try. I gradually knew enough to know how little I did know – I was unprepared to cope with children who were grieving the loss of a family member through death or marital breakdown. I gallantly tried various attempts to help a child who had spent years in a special school as a result of school phobia readjust to life in mainstream school. The children I worked with taught me that it is not easy to be seen as 'slow', 'bright', 'foreign' or 'different' in any way.

Two years spent working with children as a teacher led me to apply for a course in psychology. That course led to another, to another, to another until now regular ongoing training and development has become an important part of my life. Along the way three key influences emerged which ultimately led to my writing this book:

1   My research into the nature of stress and coping resources – what they are and how they can affect our emotions, thoughts and behaviour.
2   My training and experience in cognitive-behavioural therapy which demonstrated to me in many powerful ways that people can learn to

make sense of their distress, be helped to 'stay' with the feelings and take very definite, proactive steps to feel better.

3   My experience of working with people in many settings such as hospitals, schools, universities, families and community groups which proved again and again that the key principles of cognitive-behavioural therapy work and can be used in a very respectful way in education to help people cope with their current levels of distress as well as to prevent more serious difficulties emerging.

If any of us as adults get to the point where we need professional help with difficulties such as depression, anxiety, eating disorders, substance abuse, or even marital problems, the chances are that we will be introduced to the ideas of cognitive-behavioural therapy. Why not learn the basics of those ideas now and use them in a proactive way to help us cope with the challenges of teaching and learning?

Reading this book will give you a framework for asking yourself some key questions: 'How are you thinking and feeling about your key stressors?' 'What are you currently doing?' 'Do your feelings make sense?' 'Are your thoughts and actions "helpful" or "unhelpful"?' 'What other actions could you take which are more helpful?' If you are a teacher it makes sense that you feel under pressure at times. How you think about it and what you do about it can either increase or reduce that pressure. While you might not be able to change the particular stressor, the 'Coping Triangle' illustrates how you can become gentle towards yourself for your feelings of stress and work proactively to introduce helpful thoughts and helpful actions to make your life more relaxed and more enjoyable. Interested? Please read on!

2 Teachers, stress and the 'Coping Triangle'

How can teachers say that they are stressed and expect genuine understanding and empathy? Non-teachers view the long holidays and 'short' hours associated with teaching with envy and some even ridicule the very idea that teachers could know the meaning of a 'hard day's work'. Everyone has been to school and therefore, automatically, everyone 'knows' what a teacher's job is. Teachers can no longer look outside their profession for support and understanding, but it can be equally difficult for them to receive it within. Teachers work very much in isolation from their colleagues and can be reluctant to acknowledge to others how difficult some experiences may be. Conversations are frequently more focused on the child, rather than on the teacher's reaction to the child. Comments such as 'Johnny Smith is driving me mad – if he comes in without his homework done once more I'll ...' may be heard often. Other comments with less focus on the pupil and more on the teacher are generally not heard. How many teachers feel safe in telling their fellow teachers that 'I feel constantly annoyed with Johnny Smith and today I was so close to losing my temper with him it frightened me'?

Teaching can be a stressful job. It can be traumatic. It can be pressurised. The same, however, can be said for any job. What is important therefore is not to get stuck on proving stress, but instead understanding it and moving to do something constructive to cope with it. The following 'Stress Equation', which I devised some years ago, is a means of understanding it. Later in this chapter the focus shifts to looking in detail at what the 'Coping Triangle' is and how it works in practice to help teachers cope with their own stress, however they perceive it.

The Stress Equation:

$$S = \frac{s}{p + sup} \qquad Stress = \frac{stressor}{perception + support}$$

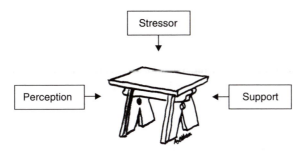

This equation is deceptively simple. Small 's' or 'stressor' is the thing which is causing us stress, 'perception' is how we interpret this to ourselves and 'support' is the internal and external supports we use.

To illustrate how the equation works, let's compare a 'big' stress with the tiniest of minor ones. The biggest stress for most of us is probably the death of someone we love. This is without doubt a huge stress resting heavily on the table. But what about the two legs supporting this stress: perception and support? In a death there is more often than not some way of perceiving some aspect of the loss in a helpful way. While we may be very angry, lonely and frightened, we may acknowledge that the person who died was in so much pain it would be cruel for us to demand them to live longer for us; or perhaps the alternative to death might have been for that person to live for a long period of time with severe brain damage; or . . . You probably know what I mean. That tiny helpful perspective may not be really acknowledged or appreciated but it is generally there all the same.

The other structure, support, is more obvious. In the immediate aftermath of the death of someone we love, there is usually great support from family, friends and even the wider community. While our ability to access this external support may be limited, it is still there. Generally we are less critical of our own internal responses at a time like this and can acknowledge that it is perfectly acceptable for us to be upset, to be numb, to be angry, to be confused and/or to be scared.

Compare this example of a very heavy stress, supported by a tiny way of looking at it helpfully and some internal and external supports available, with the following example of a tiny, minor, insignificant stressor. This example is fictitious but I think both men and women will be able to relate to it easily. It stars myself in the key role. The setting is a busy city-centre shopping street on a Saturday afternoon. The specific stressor is my noticing that there is a snag in my tights. By anyone's standards this is not really cause for concern but my reaction is to start to cry, softly at first, and then much more noticeably.

Let's use the stress definition to examine what is happening: The stressor is my noticing that my tights are snagged. How do I perceive this event? – As evidence of my stupidity. I berate myself internally with harsh criticisms: 'This is just typical – you always do something stupid like this' – 'You should have brought a spare pair' – 'You should have been more careful about where you were going.' 'And now you are howling as if the world is about to end – honestly, you are just pathetic' ...

And what about support? Well, obviously a 'damsel in distress' still motivates a 'knight in shining armour' to come to the rescue. Picture the hero stopping, very concerned, asking me to take a few deep breaths and to tell him what is upsetting me so much. Just picture his reaction when I blurt out that I have just noticed that my tights are snagged. He is very unlikely to sympathise and to offer to buy me a cup of coffee to calm me down. Instead it might be more likely for him to march off in disgust at having wasted his time, or else give me a lecture about what it is like to live in the real world and to have real problems!

So, let's compare the two situations:

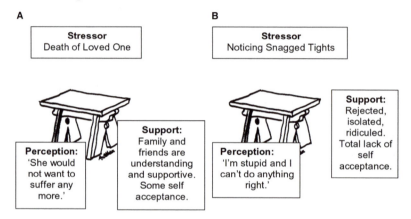

A

| Stressor |
| Death of Loved One |

Perception: 'She would not want to suffer any more.'

Support: Family and friends are understanding and supportive. Some self acceptance.

B

| Stressor |
| Noticing Snagged Tights |

Perception: 'I'm stupid and I can't do anything right.'

Support: Rejected, isolated, ridiculed. Total lack of self acceptance.

The obvious conclusion is that there must be more to situation B than we realise. Absolutely. The noticing the snagged tights incident is only one in a long, long line of tiny, insignificant stressors, which probably would not even be visible on the table above. What is important though is that in each of them I am giving myself a very hard time for being in the situation. I am being extremely self-critical and I am not allowing myself to avail of any external supports even if they are there. They may not be.

Therefore, while undoubtedly the death of someone we love is an enormous stress, it may actually add up to be a smaller overall stress than the combination of the multiple, tiny, apparently insignificant, stresses. As we know, we tend to cope with the big things in life, but it is the little things that can overwhelm us unexpectedly.

The 'Stress Equation' and the teacher

How does the 'Stress Equation' relate to the stress of teaching? Certainly teachers face big stressors all the time: pressures associated with balancing the needs of the students, with the demands of the curriculum, with the expectation of the parents. New pressures emerge on a daily basis – a child who has little English, another who has little ability, a third who has little motivation. These may be increased by lack of co-operation, apathy or outright deviance. In any class of children there are those who are not happy for reasons to do with themselves, their family or their friends. Their preoccupation may make sense but their obvious lack of interest in the particular lesson may be misinterpreted by the teacher and add to his or her overall stress.

Then there are the 'little' stresses – those tiny, almost unrecognised events that can accumulate rapidly in a teacher's day, week and life. In a primary school a small stressor may be rain determining that the children do not get a break in the fresh air but are confined to the classroom all day. A tiny stressor for a Secondary school teacher may be discovering that the previous teacher not only left the board covered with writing, but used all of the chalk or marker in doing so. Nothing big – the knock at the door interrupting the Infant teacher just as the children have started to paint; the Fifth year student arriving in late disrupting the class yet again in an exam class in Secondary school.

How might the teacher cope? At times of pressure it can be very difficult to realise that the feelings of stress, of pressure, of being totally overwhelmed are logical and make sense. Instead we can fall automatically into our patterns of coping without realising that we have actually a choice.

When I work with teachers helping them to cope with stress I first introduce them to the 'Stress Equation' as a means of identifying their own particular stressors and to help them realise that their overall sense of pressure does not come solely from one incident, but is influenced by other events as well as by their own perceptions of the event and by their ability to cope in a supportive, helpful way. I then move to introduce them to the 'Coping Triangle' to present in a logical structure the key principles of cognitive-behavioural therapy. The point of this is not specifically to make them feel less stressed and happier. At times, given the complexity of what is going on for them, feelings of desperation, isolation and distress are absolutely normal and make perfect sense. What matters most is how the person interprets the situation and what he or she does about it. Therefore the key point is to raise their awareness and understanding about what is happening, to acknowledge their feelings and to help them explore alternative ways of thinking and behaving.

The framework can be presented in a triangle format as is illustrated below. In the centre is the specific event or situation that is causing concern. At the top left apex lies the 'thoughts' box, at the top right lies the 'feelings' box and at the bottom apex lies the 'actions' box. Each of these three can influence the other, as is demonstrated by the double arrows.

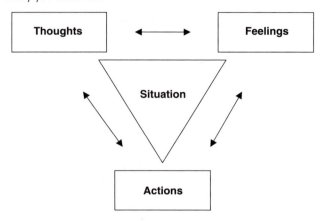

The first step in the 'Coping Triangle' is to write down as clearly as we can what our thoughts, feelings and actions are about a specific situation. The second step is to understand what feelings and thoughts are, how they can impact on each other and how they in turn can be affected by and affect actions. Generally I start with feelings, turning to focus on thoughts and finally linking both in with actions. To illustrate how thoughts affect feelings affect actions let us suppose that I am standing in a kitchen and feeling tired. I automatically put my hand onto the cooker to balance me and discover that someone has left the cooker on. What happens?

Action: I put my hand on the cooker I expect to be cold but it is hot

Feeling: Pain

Thought: 'Who left the cooker on?'

Feeling: Annoyance

Action: Shout angrily at everyone present

Feeling: Shame

Action: Apologise

Thought: 'Why am I apologising? I did not leave the cooker on'

Feeling: Annoyance at self

Thought: 'You are pathetic'

Action: Begin to berate myself.

This can be illustrated in the 'Coping Triangle' as follows:

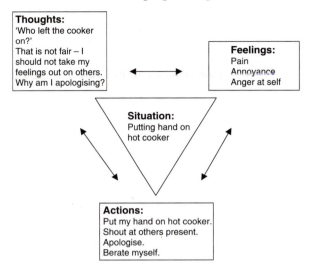

Feelings

People differ in how responsive they are to their feelings. Some have become masters at blocking or burying any uncomfortable feeling, while others scrupulously monitor each changing sensation in the body, often resulting in misinterpretation, anxiety or even terror. Feelings are simply messages to the body. That is all. The challenge is how we interpret these. If we recognise that the sick feeling in our stomach is probably linked with the fact that we have to do an interview, we probably will not pay too much attention to it. However, if we focus on our sick stomach and then allow ourselves to pay attention to thoughts such as 'My neighbour's cancer started with her feeling sick' it is likely that we will begin to feel even more anxious.

Our bodies are finely tuned instruments. Picture 'Ancestor Dan' heading out long, long ago to hunt the bear and provide food for his people. We now know that at some critical moment the body switches from 'relaxed mode' to 'action mode' and that there is a rapid increase of the hormone adrenaline in the body. Its purpose is to equip the body with the extra energy to fight or flee. Doing either of these uses up the adrenaline and the body returns naturally to its relaxed state. A third option, freezing, is also a possibility and in that case the extra adrenaline remains in the body for much longer. The adrenaline itself is not the problem. Instead, it is how it is perceived. If Dan is able to recognise that his body responds to stressful situations by increasing his adrenaline levels, he may also be more tolerant of how that feels. Some people react to it physically – they feel sick, their hearts beat faster, they want to go to the toilet, their hands are clammy, they talk too much or clam up and are not able to say a word. Just think of how you might be just before something you generally find stressful – an interview, an exam, or a dentist's appointment – and you will know what I mean.

My golden rule about feelings is: *If a feeling makes sense it is OK.* What we do about them is different. This is an important distinction, as how many of us instinctively believe that it is OK to feel jealous, miserable, mean, sneaky, cruel or wicked? Somehow, we seem to have learned that 'negative' feelings are not OK. Buddhist writers such as Pema Chödrön and Thich Nhat Hanh emphasise how important it is to stay with the feeling, no matter how difficult or uncomfortable it may be. Easier said than done, particularly when we can become so skilled in talking ourselves out of feeling 'bad'.

Over the past fifteen years I have compared people's feelings to lava in a volcano (Hayes, 2004). Instead of allowing them to flow freely, many of us stuff them into 'feeling cabinets' somewhere in our bodies, lock the drawers and possibly even throw away the keys! Some people then immediately forget that they are there and smile. Others become 'yes, but' people – they have frowns, are very pessimistic and react to any piece of good news by saying 'yes, but ...'. But what happens to the feelings? Well, just like lava, they continue to bubble until they almost seem to explode. We probably can all think of a moment when we were stunned to see the calm, easy-going person in front of us transformed into ANGER or FURY, for no apparent reason. Those feelings, which are buried very deeply, may not be allowed to explode externally and it may be some time before they surface in some form of illness.

Thoughts

Do not think of a rainbow in the sky. Now do not think of a blue boat with a red sail bobbing in the water. Lastly, do not think of a crowded classroom on a wet Friday afternoon. Were you able to 'not think', or did the images crowd in unannounced? One important point about thoughts is that they are automatic – it is almost impossible to consciously 'not think'. Thoughts in themselves are not really harmful though – the danger is when we believe them without question. Try this example: suppose at age fifteen you walked into your school corridor and you saw a group of your class-mates at the end of the corridor laughing. What might your automatic thought be? Most people immediately say 'they are laughing about me'. Perhaps they are, perhaps they are not. But if we don't question our thoughts for accuracy or for truth, we become slaves to them. Many people do not realise the power our thoughts have over us. They can evoke every type of feeling there is – from anger to sadness, joy to resentment.

Picture yourself sitting in a restaurant waiting for someone. It is now twenty minutes past the time you arranged to meet. A cartoon artist is watching you and has drawn 'thought bubbles' beside your head to illustrate what you are thinking. What would be in those bubbles? Before we can determine if our thoughts are 'helpful' or 'unhelpful' we must first catch them. This takes practice – we can be so used to not being aware of what we are thinking that initially it can come as a shock to realise how critical our thoughts may actually be. It may help to see thoughts as something external, rather than part of us – just like an aeroplane flying with a banner waving behind. We can read the message without it becoming a part of us.

Many of us do not question our thoughts at all. If we think we are fat – then we see that thought as being fact. Using the 'Coping Triangle' model we can see how that thought may trigger a feeling such as helplessness, self-disgust or determination. It may also trigger us to act in a certain way, an idea that will be developed further below.

Actions

At times actions occur so quickly it might seem as if we have no conscious control over them. They can be triggered by a thought, a feeling or by another action. We may think that someone is looking at us and we unconsciously check our appearance. We feel bored, so we start to eat. We put our hands on something hotter than we expect and we immediately pull it away. A very important point to realise is that the majority of actions are not in fact automatic, but instead are learned responses to stimuli in the form of internal or external thoughts, feelings or other actions. As actions can be helpful or unhelpful it is vital that we become aware of our behaviour. We may not be able to totally 'unlearn' behaviour, but with awareness we can certainly change it, as we will see when we look at changing the cycle. First though we need to examine the programme that directs and at times controls our thoughts, feelings and actions: our core beliefs.

Underlying core beliefs

Awareness of thoughts, feelings and actions is not enough, as hidden underneath, just like a silent computer virus, lie our core beliefs. These are what we really believe and until we become aware of them, change is very difficult. The following example illustrates how this works in practice.

Susan is extremely distressed. She has been asked to go away with her friends for the weekend, but she is afraid. Using the 'Coping Triangle' model we can see the following:

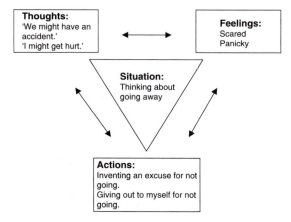

If we try to convince Susan that she will be safe and will not have an accident we will not succeed. There is actually nothing we can say which will reassure her sufficiently as in reality we cannot guarantee her safety and she knows that. Trying to convince somebody to change his or her thoughts using logic is a difficult and often unsuccessful task. Instead we can work at understanding Susan's fear by using a technique known as 'Socratic Questioning' or the 'Downward Arrow Technique' (Burns, 1980). This is how it works:

Susan

'I might have an accident.'

'What would be so bad about that?' ⇩

'I might get hurt.'

'What would be so bad about that?' ⇩

'I might have to go to hospital.'

'What would be so bad about that?' ⇩

'I might be really badly hurt.'

'What would be so bad about that?' ⇩

'I could not cope — my life would be over.'

If Susan really believes that she could not cope with the unexpected we can begin to understand how distressing the unknown can be. Core beliefs are very personal and we cannot assume that everyone's surface fear has the same underlying core belief. Several people may share Susan's fear about getting hurt, but for different reasons as we see below:

Susan	Jack	Alan
I might have an accident	I might have an accident	I might have an accident
⇩	⇩	⇩
I might get hurt	I might get hurt	I might get hurt
⇩	⇩	⇩
I might have to go to hospital	I might lose my place on the football team	People might feel sorry for me
⇩	⇩	⇩
I might be really badly hurt	I'd never get it back	They might treat me like a baby
⇩	⇩	⇩
I could not cope – my life would be over	Life without football is useless	I won't be allowed to grow up

Once we become aware of the underlying core belief we can begin to do something about it. This may be harder than we think, however, as the following story illustrates!

Traffic Attendants are Very Nice People Actually!

For years Joe had the very definite idea that traffic attendants were horrible, nasty people. In fact it was more than an idea. He really, really believed it! And because he believed it he was sure he was right and that they were horrible, nasty people. Any time he saw a tall, lean, sour traffic warden he would say to himself: 'Oh, look at that horrible mean, nasty man. He just looks so grumpy and cross.' And whenever he saw a small, chubby, grumpy traffic warden he would say 'Yes, there goes another one – another horrible, nasty, mean traffic warden!' He was always doing this and oddly enough he seemed to spot grumpy traffic wardens everywhere, even when nobody else did. He had a theory that when people who wanted to be traffic attendants went for a job and smiled or did not look horrible and mean enough they did not get the job!

Well, one day, Joe's friend was with him when they spotted two traffic attendants who were laughing and joking. 'Look Joe,' cried his friend. 'You are always talking about Traffic Attendants being horrible, nasty people, but look at those two, they're not grumpy or sour.'

But what do you think Joe said? Was it 'Oh, you're right – I must be wrong – they are not all grumpy and nasty!'?

NO!!! What he did say was 'Hmmmmm, yes, they are laughing and smiling – but that's because they have just given TEN poor people parking tickets and they are laughing!!! They are REALLY HORRIBLE, NASTY PEOPLE!!!'

The moral of the story is: we generally believe we are right and will actively seek out evidence to prove this. Anything which could possible disprove our belief is either not noticed or twisted and distorted to fit in as further proof that we are right!

Changing

In summary, feelings are messages to the body. They are triggered by external or internal cues and while the cues may be incorrect, the feelings they trigger are generally logical and make perfect sense. Difficulties arise when people become frightened by the feelings, focus on them too much or deny them altogether. Thoughts and actions are separate but can occur almost simultaneously. They can be categorised as 'helpful', 'unhelpful' or 'neutral'. Understanding that thoughts, feelings and actions are all linked and can trigger each other is an important step in changing them. It is not enough. Often when we first become aware of our thoughts we may be horrified at how many of them are critical attacks on others or ourselves. Our feelings may become understandable and we may become determined to change our behaviour. Yet, each time we resolve not to take something personally, not to fall into old, familiar patterns of behaviour, we often find ourselves having the same familiar feelings, thinking the same familiar thoughts and acting in the same familiar way. In this case awareness of this familiarity can breed contempt as we blame ourselves for being 'weak' or 'stupid' for not being able to change. Awareness at this point can actually make us feel worse about ourselves, as we consciously try to break the unhelpful cycle and fail each time.

In general, indulging in 'too much' of any behaviour is not helpful in having a balanced life – too much eating or dieting can lead to an obsession with weight and a variety of eating disorders; too much alcohol to alcoholism; too much sleep and inactivity to depression; too much worry to anxiety, and so on. While we cannot say that 'too much' automatically causes a particular difficulty, it can be enough to trigger unhelpful thoughts and/or feelings of sadness, anger, self-disgust, disappointment, regret, etc. There is nothing wrong in the feelings themselves, as we have seen, but they may in turn trigger unhelpful thoughts such as 'I hate myself for not controlling myself better' and 'I might as well eat/drink, etc. some more since I don't have the will power to stop'. These thoughts give permission to us to engage in even more of the unhelpful behaviour, and so the cycle continues, confirming all the time that our underlying beliefs are in fact correct: 'We are a failure/out of control/abandoned/insane.' As a line in a song 'No Matter What' sung by the group Boyzone (1998) says: 'What we believe is true.'

Therefore to change we must break into the cycle of thoughts/feeling/behaviour at some point. While many of us instinctively want to 'feel better', our feelings are usually a natural, understandable consequence of our thoughts and our actions. Trying to change a feeling by focusing on it generally does not work. How often have we said to students before an exam 'don't worry'? How can they do that? As soon as the thought 'don't worry' zooms into their minds, it is followed automatically by the sensation of worry. Instead we can acknowledge the feeling, understand that in the context of what we are thinking and doing it makes sense, and then become aware of exactly what we are thinking and doing – decide if our thoughts and actions are helpful or unhelpful and then work to change them. One way in which we can do this quite easily is through using the 'Coping Sentence'. This is a deceptively easy device that I developed some years ago:

'I feel ____ because ____ but ____ .'

The 'Coping Sentence' helps us to identify how we feel, link it to something which enables us to acknowledge that the feeling in itself, while it may not be comfortable, makes sense and is not wrong. The words that come after the 'but' are crucial. They must be so obviously true that they give an immediate sense of relief, rather than encouraging us to dismiss or challenge them. To say 'I feel awful because I crashed my father's car' makes sense, but to add on 'but it doesn't matter' is certainly not true or helpful. In helping a variety of people with a variety of core beliefs come up with their 'Coping Sentence' I have been fascinated by the variety and about how individual the 'but_____' must be. Two general ones 'but I'll cope' and 'but that's OK' are sometimes helpful depending on the situation. The ideal 'but___' response is one that is completely true and will always be true irrespective of the situation. An example may help in explaining what I mean. As you might guess, I have not used actual names and I am grateful to 'Jenny' and her parents for their permission to use their story as an example.

Jenny was ten when I met her to help her cope with her chronic anxiety which was interfering severely with her life as well as the lives of her younger sister, Kate (aged 5), and her parents. When I explored her thoughts, feelings and behaviour with her it was clear that Jenny was very worried that something awful might happen to her sisters and her parents. In an attempt to protect them she became so upset when her parents tried to go out at night that they actually began to stay at home rather than see her so distraught. Jenny's strategy in the school play-yard was to stand holding Kate's hand so that she would not get hurt, rather than allowing her to join in the other children's games. Using the 'Coping Triangle' Jenny was helped to understand her worry, realise that her tummy pains were a normal reaction to it, and begin to become aware of how often she had unhelpful thoughts. The final step was to bring all of this together in the 'Coping Sentence'. We discussed some possibilities, but Jenny came up with the most effective ones I have heard yet:

> '*I feel* really worried *because* Kate might fall while playing, *but it is her life.*'

> '*I feel* really worried *because* Mum and Dad might have an accident, *but it is their lives.*'

Realising that Kate and her parents had their own lives to live was a huge support to Jenny in helping her to cope with her worry.

Remember Susan, Jack and Alan who all worried that they might have an accident, but with different underlying core beliefs? Let's see how the 'Coping Sentence' can be used to help them cope:

> SUSAN: '*I feel* worried that I might have an accident *because* I think I would not be able to cope *but I keep surprising myself by how strong I actually am.*'
>
> JACK: '*I feel* worried that I might have an accident *because* I think that if I could not play football my life would be useless *but I love challenges.*'
>
> ALAN: '*I feel* worried that I might have an accident *because* I might be treated like a baby and not allowed to grow up *but I am no longer a child.*'

Two case-studies

What has all of this to do with teachers and teaching, you might ask. The remainder of this chapter takes the 'Coping Triangle' and the various ideas described above and applies them to show how two fictitious teachers, with not so fictitious difficulties, might be helped to cope.

Rachel Byrne

Rachel Byrne is three months into her first job as a newly qualified Primary School teacher. She is very dedicated and frequently spends evening and weekends preparing material for her classes. She enjoys her work and believes that she must be at her best for each child each day. She is happy with her school although at times she feels uneasy and unconfident in front of her more experienced colleagues. The Inspector from the Department of Education and Science has visited her once to discuss what she must do to be awarded her professional teaching diploma. Rachel got on well with him, but is anxious about his next visit as she knows that he will spend half a day studying her lesson plans and teaching carefully. She wonders if she was wise enrolling on a Masters in Education course so soon out of College, but wants to get all of her studying over and done with while she is young.

Stephen O'Neill

Stephen O'Neill has twenty years' experience teaching History and English. He is a very popular member of Staff in the Boys' Secondary School where he has taught since he first qualified. Increasingly he notices that one of his Sixth year students, Barry Fay, is deliberately provoking him in class. Barry's laziness and obvious disregard for authority is getting worse and other students are beginning to copy his behaviour. Stephen is frustrated that the other teachers seem to be softer on Barry and he does not accept that his difficult home circumstances should be taken into account. Numerous children see their parents separate and still manage to get their homework done on time. Stephen prides himself on his own successes and has recently begun a part-time Masters in Education in a nearby University. His philosophy in life is 'you just get on with it', and he particularly despises people who constantly look for notice and attention.

Let's suppose that Rachel and Stephen are both attending the same Masters in Education course and are asked by their lecturer to describe one incident in particular that bothered them that day. Rachel describes the situation where she was just about to do painting with her class when there was a knock at the door. It turned out to be a person from the local library who, with the Principal's permission, was touring the school telling the children about an art competition which was coming up on the theme of 'My Favourite Fairy Story'. She was delighted with her timing when she noticed the paints ready for use and suggested that they use the class to practise for the competition. Rachel was furious but said nothing until the visitor had left. Even after her second attempt to explain how to use leaves to make prints on paper, several of the children were still asking her if they could paint Cinderella, Sleeping Beauty, Goldilocks or the Three Bears. At that point she had become very cross and had practically shouted at them that she did not want to hear another word and that they were to do their work in complete silence. The frightened look on two children's faces had haunted her since and she had begun to wonder if she really did have the right temperament for teaching – maybe she was doing more harm than good and should leave teaching before she lost her temper really badly.

Stephen's reaction to her story was to nod, but to say to himself 'If she thinks that is bad it is just as well she did not opt for Secondary School teaching – she would be massacred!' He had no difficulty in describing the incident that had bothered him that day. Barely managing to contain his anger he described how Barry Fay had dared to come into his class ten minutes after the bell had gone. As he took his seat the boy had whispered something to the student beside him, which was the last straw for Stephen. He immediately asked Barry what he had said and almost exploded when he was told 'Nothing, Sir'. Determined to be fair and not make an issue of it Stephen decided to ignore this and instead asked Barry for his homework from the night before. He could see the student hesitating before he said quietly 'I don't have it with me, Sir'. Barry was very proud of his self-control and the way he asked in an interested voice 'Is it that you don't have it with you, or could it by any chance be that you actually, in fact, did not do it?' Again Barry had hesitated before saying 'Actually Sir, I did not do it'. Stephen was very aware of the total silence in the class and of the watchful, slightly hostile gaze of the other students. He barked one word 'why' and could feel his hand clenching when the boy answered in what Stephen described as a sullen voice 'I would prefer not to say, Sir'.

Stephen very quietly responded with 'Fine. If you think you can come into my class when it is half way through, sit down with no apology, or explanation to me, have a conversation with your friends, lie to me, announce that "actually" you have not bothered to do your homework, and then refuse to tell me why, I think it is better if you leave this class and don't come back. Go down to the Principal's Office and wait for me there.'

Stephen described how he had gone to the Principal Mrs Walsh's Office immediately after class to discover that Barry Fay was not there. He was just about to erupt when his Principal told him that another teacher had taken Barry to the hospital to visit his mother. She had been admitted the previous night as a result of serious blows to her head by her estranged husband. Barry had also been injured while trying to defend her, but had no serious injuries. Apparently the reason Barry was late for his History Class was that he had borrowed a friend's mobile phone and had used it in between classes to check on his mother. Mrs Walsh did not seem to see Stephen's point that it was up to Barry to have told him that. He explained that he had been calm, patient and restrained and while of course he did not like to think of any student witnessing violence, surely a teacher could not condone such overt cheek.

Let's assume that I am the lecturer in question. At this point I introduce Rachel and Stephen to the stress equation and to the 'Coping Triangle'. First they list their current stressors and then they fill in their feelings, thoughts and actions with regard to the specific thing that is bothering them.

Rachel's list of stressors might be as follows: Keeping notes up to date, being organised, being prepared, Inspector likely to be at door at any moment, trying to convince Principal even though I am young I can do the job, parents wanting me to give children more homework, three specific children in class who are particularly demanding. Stephen's list might look something like: establishing respect in the classroom, not losing face in front of students and colleagues, working to get good results with students who could not care less. Both Rachel and Stephen might also acknowledge that they have additional stressors in their personal lives such as concern over the health of a family member. While it might be helpful for them to spend some time considering their perceptions over each of these stressors as well as how they are coping with them, we will move to look at how they mapped out their thoughts, feelings and actions as illustrated below.

Rachel's 'Coping Triangle'

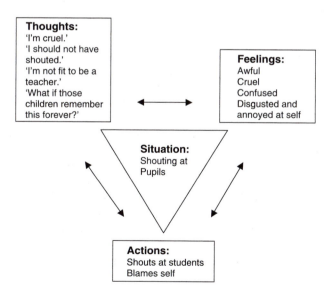

Thoughts:
'I'm cruel.'
'I should not have shouted.'
'I'm not fit to be a teacher.'
'What if those children remember this forever?'

Feelings:
Awful
Cruel
Confused
Disgusted and annoyed at self

Situation:
Shouting at Pupils

Actions:
Shouts at students
Blames self

Stephen's 'Coping Triangle'

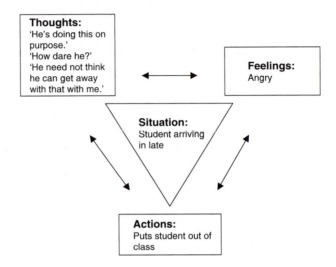

At this point Rachel and Stephen are asked if they notice anything from what they have written. Rachel is likely to be feeling a bit anxious while Stephen is probably still feeling that he is perfectly justified in being angry. They are then 'taught' about feelings as described early in this chapter, i.e. that they are internal messages and that 'if a feeling makes sense it is OK'. Therefore, while the feeling of guilt, anger, worry, etc. might not be nice or comfortable, it is more helpful for us to acknowledge the feeling and then to move to look at how we are thinking and what we are doing.

It is clear that Rachel and Stephen are both thinking in an unhelpful way. Rachel is helped to look more closely at her thoughts and to determine the extent to which she truly believes that she is cruel, should not have shouted, is not fit to be a teacher. She is also helped to look at what is the worst thing about the thought that the children might remember her shouting forever. This process uncovers Rachel's beliefs that she is completely responsible for the future well-being of the children in her class, and that to be a good teacher she must be perfect. At this stage Rachel may recognise that these beliefs are irrational and are causing her undue distress and pressure.

Stephen's thoughts are different and rather than being self-critical like Rachel's are directed outwards. It may not be particularly helpful to try and persuade him that his student, Barry Fay, may not in fact be deliberately trying to cause trouble. Stephen clearly believes that this is the case and therefore is angry. His anger makes sense, but may only be sparked, rather than caused, by Barry's behaviour. In asking Stephen what is so bad about Barry doing this on purpose and continuing that line of questioning in a Downward Arrow Technique as described above, he may reveal the following insights into his core beliefs:

Stephen

He is doing this on purpose

What is so bad about that?   ⇩

The other students are
watching

What is so bad about that?   ⇩

They will think I cannot handle
the situation

What is so bad about that?   ⇩

They will think I am too soft

What is so bad about that?   ⇩

Soft people get walked on

It would be very interesting to explore with Stephen where his belief that 'soft people get walked on' originates. It may have something to do with his own relationship with his parents, his siblings, or his own school days. The chances are that this belief was formed a long time ago as a reaction to something. Perhaps he witnessed a friend being bullied and ridiculed in the schoolyard and decided that he would never allow himself to be 'weak'. While it may be interesting, it is not essential for Stephen to know when and why he developed this belief. Instead, understanding that he does believe it can help him reflect on why it is that he has always had such a strong reaction to boys like Barry Fay. Could it be that he perceives those teachers who are kind and understanding to Barry's particular difficulties as 'soft' and are leaving themselves open to being 'walked on'?

Helping Rachel and Stephen cope with their feelings involves helping them to become aware of their thoughts and beliefs, as we have seen above. This is not enough, however. They must also become aware of their behaviours, of how they act and react in different situations. This might involve both of them learning some basic relaxation techniques as soon as they become aware that they are feeling anxious or angry. One simple but effective exercise is for them to tighten their left hand into a tight fist while at the same time breathing in. They then hold their breath for three seconds before releasing the breath and their hands. If they practise this in cycles of three, it means that as well as having something concrete to do as a means of distraction, they also are allowing themselves to become calmer. Other helpful actions may involve talking to somebody trusted about their worries;

developing a healthy lifestyle in terms of eating habits, exercise, rest and sleep; expressing their emotions in healthy ways such as sport, journal writing or art.

It might take a little time to work out the most appropriate and effective 'Coping Sentence' but it is worth the effort. In the context of the two case studies described above we can see how helpful the following 'Coping Sentences' could be in helping to prevent or reduce future distress:

> RACHEL: '*I feel* awful *because* I lost my temper with the children in my class and I think they might be scarred for life, *but I am learning to relax.*'
>
> STEPHEN: '*I feel* furious *because* I think that Barry was deliberately goading me *but I am the adult in the classroom.*'

The following chapter develops the various ideas described above in the context of the child. It examines some of the general factors that may be involved in a girl or boy developing certain core beliefs about themselves and others such as gender, birth order, intelligence, personality and age. The focus then moves to look at how teachers can use this information in a practical, respectful way to help themselves and their pupils cope with the 'normal' challenges, which is essential before moving to consider the specific issues of anger, anxiety and depression which are discussed later.

3 Common stressors in the classroom: Age, gender, ability and personality

This book is aimed at helping teachers gain relief from stress. It might be very simplistic, and perhaps not too popular, to say that teachers bring stress on themselves. Many of us would much prefer to blame the students! However, this chapter looks at how teachers' beliefs about the effects of factors such as age, gender, ability and personality can at times impact on them in a way which adds to their stressors and which can reduce their overall ability to cope. The 'Stress Equation' and the 'Coping Triangle' are used to demonstrate how teachers can become aware of the nature of their stress and the key role their own perception of this plays and how they can then work to cope in a more helpful, responsible way. The focus is initially on the possible impact of teachers' beliefs towards their students, but moves to look at how age, gender, ability and personality may also be key stressors. The chapter concludes with a true example to illustrate how the 'Coping Triangle' was successful in helping one student teacher become aware of and overcome his fears about teaching children he perceived to be 'very bright'.

Before we go any further I would like you to do some detective work to discover your thoughts and feelings as well as what you generally do in relation to students. Think of the student you have most enjoyed teaching since your very first time entering the classroom. See him/her in your mind as clearly as you possibly can. Now complete the following exercise:

Exercise 3.1

> .... is the student I have most enjoyed teaching. My favourite moment teaching him/her happened when he/she was ... . years old. Briefly this was to do with .... I remember him/her as being a very .... student who found school-work .... The best way to describe his/her personality is to say that he/she was ....

Now, take a few moments to think of the one student who stands out in your mind as being the complete opposite – the student you hated teaching. Again, see him/her in your mind as clearly as you possibly can and complete the following exercise:

Exercise 3.2

> .... is the student I have least enjoyed teaching. My worst moment teaching him/her happened when he/she was .... years old. Briefly this was to do with .... I remember him/her as being a very .... student who found school-work .... The best way to describe his/her personality is to say that he/she was ....

Now get four sheets of paper. Divide each in half horizontally and draw out two 'thoughts/feelings/actions' triangles on each page. Take the top half of each page to list your thoughts, etc. about the student you most enjoyed teaching, while the bottom half is for the student you least liked teaching. Next place each student's gender, age, ability and personality in the centre of the triangles and complete the 'thoughts, feelings and actions' boxes.

Borrowing a phrase from cookery programmes 'here are some fictitious examples I prepared earlier':

Joan Fallon (Maths teacher with ten years' experience)

Mike Daly is the student I have most enjoyed teaching. My favourite moment teaching him happened when he was thirteen years old. Briefly this was to do with his quick wit in using a mathematical equation to back up his theory of homework being a waste of time. I remember him as being a very capable, willing student who found school-work easy. The best way to describe his personality is to say that he was a very alert, friendly, easygoing boy who had a great sense of humour and who related well to his teachers as well as his peers.

Laura White is the student I have least enjoyed teaching. My worst moment teaching her happened when she was sixteen years old. Briefly this was to do with her complete refusal to participate in the class and her challenging me to make her. I remember her as being a very stubborn, troublesome student who found school-work boring. The best way to describe her personality is to say that she was a self-centred, spoiled young woman who had no consideration for her teachers or her class-mates.

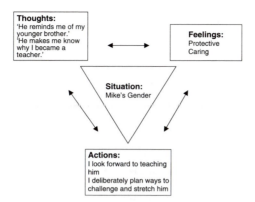

Figure 3.1 Joan's reactions to Mike's gender

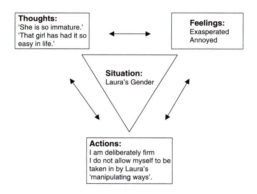

Figure 3.2 Joan's reactions to Laura's gender

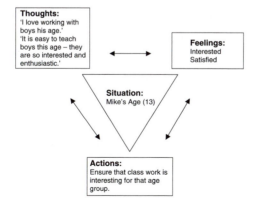

Figure 3.3 Joan's reactions to Mike's age

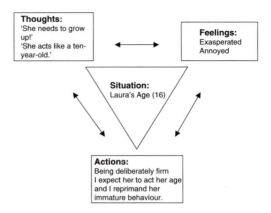

Figure 3.4 Joan's reactions to Laura's age

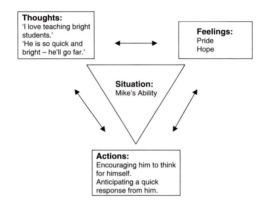

Figure 3.5 Joan's reactions to Mike's ability

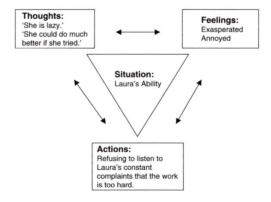

Figure 3.6 Joan's reactions to Laura's ability

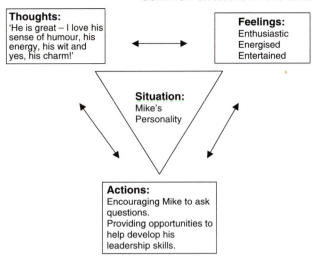

Figure 3.7 Joan's reactions to Mike's personality

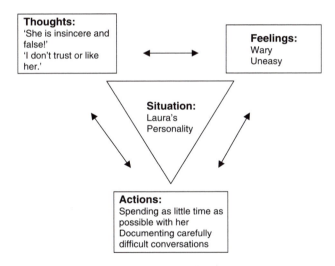

Figure 3.8 Joan's reactions to Laura's personality

What are your own thoughts and feelings at this point? Do you think that Joan is being unfair to Laura? If so, do you feel aggrieved or even angry? Perhaps you are reminded of a student you once taught who seems to be very like Laura – perhaps you are thinking that you may have been unfair to him/her and if so, you might feel some guilt or shame. Do you feel that Joan is being naive in her response to Mike, or perhaps being very unfair to Mike's classmates? As we have seen in the previous chapter, how we think affects how we feel, which in turn affects what we do. We will examine a little closer Joan's own reaction to this exercise, but for you to get maximum benefit from it I suggest that you first complete the following exercises:

Exercise 3.3 My reactions to Joan's reaction to Mike

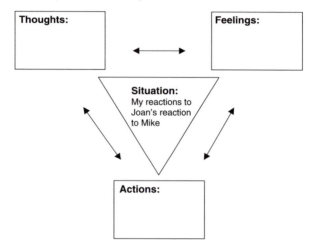

Exercise 3.4 My reactions to Joan's reaction to Laura

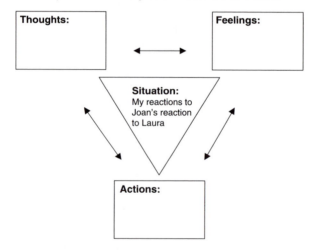

What have you learned from doing those two exercises? Did you notice yourself identifying with Joan, or being totally repulsed by her reaction to one or both of the students?

Once Joan had completed the two triangles my next step would be to help her to become aware of her underlying beliefs as a means of understanding her reactions to both students. Remember how Joan described Mike and Laura?

> Mike: 'a very capable, willing student who found school-work easy ... a very alert, friendly, easygoing boy who had a great sense of humour ... he related well to his teachers as well as his peers'.

> Laura: 'a very stubborn, troublesome student who found school-work boring ... she was a self-centred, spoiled young woman who had no consideration for her teachers or her classmates'.

Is Joan right in her analysis of Mike and Laura, or could she possibly be influenced by underlying beliefs she might not even know exist?

If I were working with Joan I would move the focus away from Mike and Laura as individuals to allow her room to explore underlying beliefs about gender, age, ability and personality. Her reactions to Mike initially might seem ideal for a teacher to have (we will look at this later), but then why does she react so differently to Laura? Many of you reading this might empathise with Joan completely and perhaps feel some degree of anger towards me for even suggesting that there may be something 'wrong' in Joan's reaction. This book is not about 'right' and 'wrong'. In a nutshell it is about shifting our focus as teachers from saying to our colleagues and ourselves:

> 'Steve Adams is driving me crazy – if he comes in without his homework done once more I will scream' to

> 'There is something about Steve Adams' habit of not doing his homework which is really bothering me.'

In the first situation the teacher places the responsibility for being 'driven crazy' onto a child in the class; in the second, the teacher is aware that it is her reaction to his behaviour, rather than the behaviour itself, which needs to be looked at.

There is clearly something about Laura that bothers Joan. It is not enough to say that a child like Laura would bother anyone. Teachers have a duty of care towards every child, not just the ones they like and who make them feel good about themselves. So let us explore Joan's reactions to Laura further. She completed the exercises above each time contrasting her thoughts, feelings and actions to Laura, with her reactions to Mike. Table 3.1 contains her reactions to Laura only. What are your own thoughts and feelings as you read them again?

Using the 'Coping Triangle' I would help Joan look at her feelings to Laura – exasperation, annoyance, wariness, and uneasiness. Do these feelings make sense given what she is thinking and what she is doing in relation to Laura? Yes, I would think so. It might be helpful for Joan to reflect on other situations where her typical response is exasperation and

Table 3.1 Joan's reactions to Laura

	Feelings	Thoughts	Actions
Gender	Exasperated Annoyed	She is so immature That girl has had it so easy in her life	Being deliberately firm Not allowing myself to be taken in by her manipulating ways
Age	Exasperated Annoyed	She is so immature That girl has had it so easy in her life	Being deliberately firm Not allowing myself to be taken in by her manipulating ways
Ability	Exasperated Annoyed	She is lazy She could do much better if she tried	Refusing to listen to Laura's constant complaint that the work is too hard.
Personality	Wary Uneasy	She is insincere and false. I don't trust or like her.	Spending as little time as possible with her. Documenting carefully 'difficult' conversations.

annoyance, but for now acknowledging that her feelings make sense to her is enough. So, let us move on to what she is thinking. My guess is that Joan will defend her thoughts vigorously – asking her to list all of the ways in which Laura is 'mature' or has had a tough life will not, in my experience, work. Remember the Traffic Warden story? Instead, we might take each of Joan's thoughts in turn and ask the question 'Is this thought helpful or unhelpful?' She might immediately respond by telling us that the thought 'she is so immature' is neither helpful nor unhelpful, but is true. That might be so (or indeed might be a belief that Joan has!) but let us suppose that I am doing a 24 hour fast for charity – the thought 'I am hungry' might be true, but if I repeatedly tell myself that I am hungry, the thought quickly becomes unhelpful.

If we turn on a light switch, we may get light. If we turn on an electric cooker we may get heat generated by electricity. If we turn on a gas cooker we may get heat generated by gas. We all know that and most times do not stop to wonder at how this actually happens. It just does. We generally only stop to wonder about it when something is faulty and does not work. Do you see the connection? Joan thinks 'she is so immature' and 'that girl has had it so easy in her life' and feels exasperated and annoyed. A reaction that occurs so quickly is just like turning on a light switch and getting light. We think angry thoughts and we feel angry. Is this helpful for Joan? I would say 'no' and that is why I consider her thoughts unhelpful. 'But why,' someone might ask, 'do those thoughts generate feelings of exasperation and annoyance?' Yes, someone else might have the same thoughts and feel envy, humour or perhaps sadness. We need to look at the underlying core beliefs to understand why those thoughts create feelings of annoyance and exasperation for Joan. Let's use the Socratic Questioning Technique we saw in Chapter 2.

Joan

She is so immature

'What is so bad about that?' ⇩

She does not have a clue about life

'What is so bad about that?' ⇩

She thinks she can just do what she wants

'What is so bad about that?' ⇩

She doesn't care about other people

'What is so bad about that?' ⇩

Other people have to pick up the pieces

'What is so bad about that?' ⇩

Other people suffer

'Other people suffer.' That could very easily be the 'bottom line' response to Joan's thought 'That girl has had it so easy in her life'. At this point it might be helpful for Joan to gently reflect on times in her life when she 'suffered' as a result of someone else's immature behaviour. Yes, Freud did have it right when he emphasised the incredible power of the unconsciousness. If Joan does not realise that her own experience of being the eldest child who was held responsible for the 'immature behaviour' of her younger twin sisters has in some ways affected her, how could she possibly connect her own feelings of 'exasperation' and 'annoyance' towards a child like Laura? And what hope could Laura ever have of convincing Joan that actually she is a nice kid, with a lot of strengths?

So, are we now in the business of 'analysing' every teacher's childhood? No – just our own! The more aware we are of our own particular buttons, the more we can take responsibility for our reactions to other people and situations. It is not Laura who has caused Joan's feelings – instead it is Joan's reactions to Laura, and yes, often these reactions do go back to our own childhoods.

Let us develop this idea a little more by looking at what Joan can learn from her reaction to Mike, as summarised in Table 3.2.

Table 3.2 Joan's reactions to Mike

	Feelings	*Thoughts*	*Actions*
Gender	Protective Caring	He reminds me of my younger brother. He makes me know why I became a teacher	Looking forward to teaching him. Deliberately planning ways to challenge and stretch him
Age	Interest Satisfaction	I love working with boys his age. It is so easy to teach them They are interested and alive	Ensuring that class work is interesting for that age group
Ability	Pride Hope	I love teaching bright students. He is so quick and bright – he'll go far.	Encouraging him to think for himself. Anticipating a quick response from him.
Personality	Enthusiastic Energised Entertained	He is great – I love his sense of humour, his energy, his wit and yes, his charm!	Encouraging Mike to ask questions. Providing opportunities to help him develop his leadership skills.

Clearly Joan enjoys teaching Mike. He reminds her of her younger brother and makes her feel good about herself as a teacher. Adapting the Socratic questioning style a little we can help her explore why this might be so.

Joan	He reminds me of my younger brother
Claire 'What is so good about that?'	⇩
Joan	He cares about me!

Can you see Joan's amazement as she quickly makes the connection between her feelings towards her younger brother and her student Mike? She realises that her experiences of growing up two years older than twin sisters may have resulted in her feeling overly responsible, 'blamed', excluded and resentful. Her way of coping was to describe them as 'being immature' and to relish and value her own maturity. Her brother Mike was born when she was eight. Her younger sisters had no time for him and were 'too immature' to look after him anyway. Joan absolutely adored him from the first moment she saw him, but had no idea about how much she depended on his 'hero-worshipping' her to make her feel good about herself. It suddenly made sense to her why she enjoyed teaching boys like Mike and absolutely hated with a passion teaching girls like Laura. Actually, now that she thought about it a little she realised how little she enjoyed teaching girls anyway.

Perhaps that level of awareness would be enough to help Joan understand her feelings, thoughts and actions towards her students. Before we look in more detail at the effect of her behaviour, using the 'Coping Triangle', let us just explore a little further her core belief that other people suffer from immature behaviour. Many people share the view that we react in a particularly negative way to those aspects of our own selves we do not accept, or like. Joan's own tendency to behave in an 'immature' way may be hidden very deeply, but it is there. We could use the Socratic questioning technique again and this time might explore why Joan might behave in a way she hates so much. It is easy to see then why she might be so attacking, critical and judgemental of herself in situations where she perceives herself to be 'immature'. The simple truth is that the more relaxed and accepting she becomes of her own 'immature tendencies' the less critical and judgemental she will be of others.

Students are the best teachers that teachers will ever have. It takes courage to turn the spotlight inwards and question our own responses and reactions to students rather than to automatically blame them. It takes courage, but it also needs immense amounts of gentleness towards ourselves. What help is it going to be to anyone if in the process of harsh and maybe even savage critical, judgemental self-reflection we condemn ourselves to suffer even further? Very often I find that people who are extremely critical towards others are actually much more critical towards themselves. Becoming aware of this critical aspect of ourselves in a gentle, accepting way can be incredibly difficult. We will consider how we might do this as well as how we might help our students do this when we look at depression in a later chapter.

For now, my suggestion to Joan would be that she looks again at her reactions to Laura using the 'Coping Triangle'. She now realises that her feelings towards both Laura and Mike make sense, given her own particular background. Bottling up her annoyance and resentment is clearly not helpful, so Joan might decide to look, in a very gentle way, at her underlying feelings towards her sisters and her brother. Her thoughts towards Laura are not helpful either, as they automatically switch the 'exasperation' and 'annoyance' feeling switches. Joan cannot immediately change her feelings towards children like Laura. Nor can she rid her head of all of those unhelpful thoughts. Instead, she can use the 'Coping Sentence' to acknowledge her feelings, deliberately choose to think 'helpful' thoughts and to act in a strong helpful way. We have not explored how Joan has typically responded to Laura and Mike, but even a cursory glance tells us that her actions towards Laura have typically been unhelpful and are in marked contrast to her behaviour towards Mike. The very good news for Joan is that she loves teaching, is a great teacher towards students like Mike and just needs to work on extending that towards students who make her feel more uneasy and apprehensive.

Coming up with a 'but' for the 'Coping Sentence' generally takes a little time and effort. The 'but' must be true, it must be strong and it must be something that the person can relate to immediately and can use in all situations. Some examples for Laura might be:

'I feel <u>exasperated</u> because <u>I think that Laura is so immature</u> (given Joan's history with her own sisters that makes sense) ***but maybe this is more about me than her.***'

'I feel <u>annoyed</u> because <u>I think that Laura could do much better if she tried</u> (if she thinks this, it makes sense that she might feel annoyed) ***but I choose to be the best teacher I can be for all of my students.***'

'I feel <u>wary</u> because <u>I think that Laura is insincere and false</u> (again wariness seems to be an understandable reaction to this thought) ***but I choose to give her the benefit of the doubt.***'

Awareness can be powerful. Here is an exercise that can demonstrate just how powerful! Choose a picture (on the wall, or in a children's book) that has plenty of colours in it. Give the following instructions to some willing volunteers: 'In a moment I am going to ask you to look at this picture for three seconds and tell me what is red.' Allow them three seconds to examine the picture and then say: 'What was white?' The chances are that they will initially look stunned and may say: 'But I only looked at red!' The next step is to ask: 'If I was to show you that picture again and this time ask you to tell me what was blue, would you do it the same way as you did a moment ago, or would you do it differently?' Most people would immediately say that they would do it differently – they would now look at the whole picture, instead of just focusing on one colour! You then explain that you tricked them, and now that they are aware that it was a trick, they will not allow themselves to be caught out again – awareness has changed their behaviour! It only takes an instant to change, and yet the effects can last forever. I have never been able to fool anyone twice on that exercise. The change can be so definite that even a simple request to ask someone to pick up a pen can be met with a 'what does she really want?' reaction. That is great as it proves how just being aware can change behaviour. I have seen people make incredible progress changing patterns of behaviour that they have had for years when they suddenly realise they are no longer helpful to them.

Awareness is an essential first step to coping successfully with situations and students you have previously found difficult. My hope is that you are now aware that your reactions to the students you teach is due in part to your own beliefs, thoughts, feelings and behaviour. These, as we have seen above, often make sense, but may be unhelpful for us and for the students we teach. We can learn to think and act differently and this in turn can help us to feel differently and to get much more satisfaction from our work. Of course awareness with understanding is even better. Without sufficient understanding of the origin of our own beliefs we can become overly self-critical and judgemental. With understanding can come compassion and gentleness. It is logical then that understanding our selves and the various roles we have in life can help us become better teachers. Why have we chosen to be teachers? Was it to please our parents? To follow in the path of a teacher we admired greatly? Did it grow from a determination to be a better teacher than the ones who tried, but failed, to teach us? Is it because we have a genuine desire to share in the magic of children's growth and development? Or is it the more cynical, but for many real, reasons of 'June, July and August'? Are the reasons we chose to become teachers still valid and alive today, or have they been replaced by other, less satis-fying reasons?

Teachers' beliefs about their own age, gender, ability and personality

The focus of this chapter until now has been to raise your awareness to the power of your own beliefs regarding the students you teach. I would ask you to take a few moments to reflect on your beliefs about the effects of your own age, gender, ability and personality and to ascertain if these beliefs are actually stressors in their own right! Your responses to Exercise 3.5 below might surprise you!

Exercise 3.5 My beliefs about the effects of my age, gender, ability and personality on my role as teacher

Age	I am .... years old.
	This means that I am one of the .... teachers in the school.
	Being my age ... (is/is not) an advantage because ....
	Because of my age the other teachers ....
	I believe that being my age is .... in my teaching with
	the students as they ....
	Finally, I believe that my age ....
Gender	I am a ....(man/woman).
	This .... (has/has not) an(y) impact on my role as teacher because ....
	....
	Students see male teachers as .... and female teachers as
	....
	Finally, I believe that my gender ....
Ability	It is .... years since I qualified as a teacher.
	I believe that my ability as a teacher is ....
	Other teachers in the school consider me to be a .... teacher.
	I .... (worry/don't worry) about my ability to teach.
	Finally, I believe that my ability ....
Personality	I am .... type of person.
	This means that as a teacher I ....
	Other teachers in the school describe me as ....
	I think my personality ... (is/is not) suited to the role of teacher because
	....
	Finally, I believe that my personality ....

It would be a very interesting exercise for you to ask one or more of your colleagues to complete Exercise 3.5 as if they were you!

This chapter now concludes with a story to illustrate how a young student teacher's beliefs about his own intellectual abilities directly impacted on his ability to teach. This is a true story. I have his parents' permission to tell it, as tragically their son, Peter, died from cancer during his second year as a Secondary School teacher. When he was training to be a teacher I was one of the supervisors of his teaching practice. On my first visit to him I sat at the back of the classroom and witnessed the best class I have ever seen a student teach. The subject was History and Peter's students were in the lowest stream according to ability. He brought History to life in the most creative, magical way possible. It was a privilege to share in the excitement and enthusiasm of the students. As I had time, I decided to stay and observe Peter's next class, Geography, to students in the highest stream. The contrast could not be more marked and I was so glad that I had seen the History class first. Peter stood, anxious, in front of a group of bored young adolescents. His voice was low, he kept his head down, concentrating solely on the textbook and was clearly relieved when the bell went announcing the end of that class period.

Our conversation exploring what had happened was fascinating. Peter was very aware of the difference in his performance and began to blame himself and to apologise. When we looked at the contrast between the two classes I had observed, and at what had made the remarkable difference in his teaching, his underlying core belief that he was 'no good teaching bright students' became clear. Peter explained that he loved teaching students who struggled to learn. He knew what that meant as he said he had struggled to learn through his own days as a student. He felt relaxed and at ease with the 'weaker' students and did not feel that they were judging him. He could be himself.

When we used the 'Coping Triangle' model to explore what happened each time he taught the brighter students the pattern in Figure 3.9 emerged.

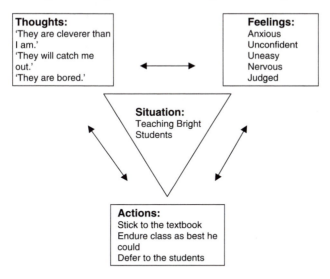

Figure 3.9 Peter's reactions to teaching 'bright' students

When we explored Peter's pattern, his feelings of anxiety made sense given his nervousness when faced with the more able students. He identified his own thoughts as unhelpful and was very interested to notice how his actions differed so completely from his actions when he was teaching the classes he loved. I encouraged him to bring his talent and his creativity into his teaching with students in the higher streams and to challenge his own thoughts that they might think his use of concrete visual aids as silly. We worked on a 'Coping Sentence' which would help him acknowledge how he felt, make sense of it and give him a boost of confidence. The one that worked was:

> 'I feel <u>nervous</u> because <u>I am about to teach the students in the top stream</u> *but I am very well prepared.*'

Peter decided to take the same History class I had observed and teach it to the higher stream students and was delighted to discover that they responded to his creativity and his enthusiasm just as much as those in the lower stream had done. It was no surprise that Peter got an A grade in his teaching practice. The school in which he did his teaching practice offered him a job before he had his exam results and during the two years he taught there he earned the deep respect of his students, their parents and his colleagues. He also earned the well-deserved reputation of being an 'excellent teacher'. Peter started his teaching career preferring to teach those students who struggled to learn. When he realised that his own lack of confidence was a key factor, he took steps to develop his teaching skills to benefit all students, irrespective of their abilities.

This chapter examined how our own beliefs of students' ability, age, gender and personality can impact on how we teach and can be everyday stressors. Our beliefs about our own ability, age, gender and personality are also important and can also become extra stressors. Chapter 4 considers three very common reactions that teachers and students can have to such stressors – anger, anxiety and/or depression – and demonstrates how the 'Coping Triangle' can be used to help relieve the underlying stress.

4   Anger, anxiety and depression as reactions to stress

Take a few moments to consider how you normally react to stress. Do you tend to clench your fist tightly and deliberately work at speaking calmly and slowly, conscious that you really want to lash out and fight? Do you feel the tension in your stomach but smile and pretend it is not there? Or do you consider the stress as confirmation that all is not right with you, your future and the world around you, and withdraw a little more from others? How do you react to extreme stress? What words do you usually use to describe your reaction? 'I was completely furious'? 'I was sick with anxiety'? 'I was so depressed I did not care what happened'? As we have seen, words are very powerful. The meaning of the event, rather than the event itself, determines our reactions, and this meaning is usually described in words.

The human reaction to stress is complex and varied. Naturally there can be a variety of emotions such as disappointment, exhilaration, guilt, shame, hope and pride that can be experienced simultaneously in our response to difficult situations. I have chosen just three emotions to focus on in this chapter: anger, anxiety and depression. This is not intended to minimise the importance of any of the other emotions, but anger, anxiety and depression are certainly three very common reactions to severe stress. As they can also become serious stressors in their own right, and can contribute to the conditions of anxiety and depression, it makes sense that understanding them is essential in relieving stress.

The first step is to understand the power of the labels behind the words 'angry', 'anxious' and 'depressed'. Would you naturally say, 'She is angry'? 'She is anxious'? 'She is depressed'? I know that many people feel that there is no real difference between describing someone as 'depressed' or 'having depression'. There is a huge difference to me. To illustrate this I have written below a summary of how I used to explain the difference between 'being a diabetic' and 'having diabetes' to children and their parents. As you read it, consider again how you habitually describe people – is it 'she is ...' or 'she has ...'?

The power of labels

Part of my work in a Children's Hospital some years ago was as a clinical psychologist working on a multi-disciplinary team to help children with diabetes cope. I saw a key element of my job at that time as helping children, their parents and families and often the medical staff to consider their perceptions and beliefs of the disease, and if necessary to change these. Please take a moment to consider how you generally describe that disease. Is it normal for you to say that a child 'is a diabetic' or do you automatically say he 'has diabetes'? Do you see any difference between these two ways of describing it? As you may have guessed, I favour the 'has diabetes' approach. The following pictures are shown to illustrate how I used to explain my reason for this to children, and more particularly to the key adults in their lives.

This little person here can be taken to be the child before the illness is diagnosed.

This is just after the child has been diagnosed. He is looking a little puzzled and unsure. Childhood diabetes is for life. It involves injections, careful diet and is not nice!

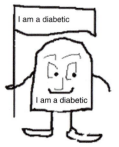

Now he has a choice about how to explain the illness to himself and to others. He can decide to incorporate it into his identity and become a diabetic, so that very quickly, the fact that he is a diabetic is one of the most important things about him.

He has another option though. He can consider that he has been given a bag to carry for the rest of his life, which has diabetes.

At this point I generally explain to parents why I prefer the 'I have approach'.

As soon as the child begins to think of himself as 'a diabetic', he begins to be considered by everyone else as that. Being a diabetic becomes his identity and can become the most important fact about him. This way of thinking makes it very difficult to dislike or reject any part of the disease, as to do so then involves rejecting himself.

If the child chooses to consider that he 'has' rather than 'is' the disease, he can keep his own identity separate. He has blue eyes, green shoes and diabetes. The bag image can be very helpful for parents as initially they help the doctors and nurses carry the bag for him. Very quickly, they begin to carry it on their own, allowing him to learn how to carry some of it from a very early age.

Remember the importance of meaning! We can substitute the words 'diabetic' with practically any label. What does it mean to us as teachers to have a child in our class with the label 'angry', 'worried', or 'sad'? What does it mean for us when we react to a situation in an angry, anxious or depressed way? Notice what thoughts are in your head as you read the 'Lunchtime in the Staff-Room' story. (It is fictitious of course!)

Lunchtime in the Staff-Room

It was Wednesday lunchtime. The staff-room was full and the attention of everyone present was focused on a discussion four of the teachers were having about a particular football match the evening before. Those not directly involved realised that three of the teachers were having some good-natured fun with the fourth, who was very upset because the Referee had sent two men off the pitch unfairly. 'Honestly,' said the irate teacher, 'it was just like being forced to watch our Principal, Joe, making another bad decision disciplining two students and not being able to do anything.' This remark was met with gales of laughter, as those present knew exactly how frustrating their Principal's easygoing style with the students could be. In the midst of their merriment, the door opened and immediately everyone present stopped laughing. They held their breath hoping that the person entering was not Joe.

Let's pause at this point in the story and consider that the person coming in was another teacher, Anita. What do you think her most likely automatic thought will be when she opens the door and hears laughter that immediately stops? The chances are she will think that everyone in the entire staff-room was talking about her. This thought will then very quickly trigger feelings such as anger, anxiety and/or sadness. Just see yourself in her position – how do you think you would feel and what would you do? Some of us might pretend that we did not notice – others might react in a very aggressive, sarcastic way, while someone else might interpret it as further evidence that they are unpopular and that their colleagues are not supportive and friendly. Why? What makes the difference between a very easy, calm 'Hello there, what's the joke?' to 'I hate teaching in this school – I can trust noone' type of response? Obviously, it is not so much the sudden silence as the door opens, but rather the meaning of this sudden silence to the person entering. This meaning, as we have seen, is personal and depends on a range of factors including the health of the person, the number of stressors she is currently coping with, her perception of the silence and her own resilience in coping with this.

But let us continue with the story for a few moments considering four possible endings:

> In the midst of their merriment, the door opened and immediately everyone present stopped laughing. They held their breath hoping that the person entering was not Joe.

1   'Hello there, what's the joke? – Oh, don't tell me you were complaining about poor Joe again. Honestly, that man cannot do anything right. OK, what has he done now?'
2   'Do you know – that is the last straw. I am so sick and tired of coming into this staff-room and noticing that the room goes silent every time I enter. It is horrible and

I have had enough of it. In future I am going to eat my lunch in my car.'

3 'Excuse me, Janet, do you mind if I whisper to you as I don't want the others to hear me – but I was wondering, why did everyone stop laughing when I came in? Were they laughing about me? Have I done something I did not realise? Why did nobody tell me before? How long has it been going on for?'

4 'Don't mind me – continue with your joke. I am going to go over here and read the paper.'

Now, a tough question perhaps. Which of the four is most likely to be your automatic response? Or would you react differently?

Let's suppose that lunchtime is over and that Anita walks in to teach her class, notices that three of the students are huddled in a group discussing something intently and look up with what Anita considers to be a guilty look when she walks in. What immediately goes through her head? Well, it is probably fair to say that this will be influenced by her experience in the staff-room and she might say one of the following:

1 'Hmm, more "hush-hush" conversations. All right Students, settle down and let's get started for class.'

2 'This is ridiculous. I am so tired of whispering everywhere I go. Do you have no idea of how tiring your behaviour can be? I have had enough of this and I do not think I want any of you in my class today. I will give you one last chance but you are to move to your seats NOW – I said NOW – OK, Michael Mooney, if you are going to continue to look at me in that defiant way I have no choice but to send you to the Principal. OK, that is it – I have had enough – go now, please. NOW. Pardon, Mr Ford, did I actually hear you mutter that that is not fair? Well, if you think it is so unfair that Mr Mooney has to face the Principal on his own, I think it might be better if you go along with him – NOW – All right, is there anyone else in this class who wants to leave? Fine, books out then.'

3 'Erm, excuse me for a moment. I want to check something with the teacher next door'...'Tony, excuse me, is there anything odd about my appearance today? I know you are just about to start teaching, but I just wondered if ... Oh, right, thank you!'

4 'Don't mind me – continue with your scheming – but please let me know when you are ready to start.'

What has happened? Situation One is self-explanatory and is possibly how we would prefer to react to stressful situations – acknowledge them, not take them personally and move on. Let's examine each of the other reactions, using the 'Coping Triangle', and see how angry, anxious or depressed reactions can become stressors in their own right (see Figures 4.1, 4.2 and 4.3).

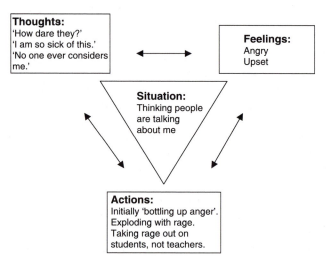

Figure 4.1 Angry response

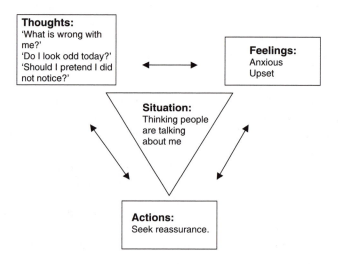

Figure 4.2 Anxious response

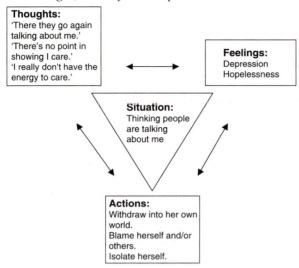

Figure 4.3 Depressed response

Obviously every person can react to a situation calmly, angrily, anxiously or in a depressed way depending on many variables, such as the particular meaning of the event to her and how tired and/or hungry she is. It is very important to note that our reactions can also be learned responses to a particular stimulus or situation. Our ways of responding may be so fast, we may not realise that we are actually on 'automatic pilot'. Chapter 8 presents a summary of learning theory and reminds us of the contributions of people like Pavlov, Skinner and Bandura, as well as the more recent inputs of Beck and Ellis. For now it is enough to remind ourselves of the power of stimulus-response. Have a look at the words on the left column in Exercise 4.1 and as quickly as you can, without thinking too much about the exercise, write down your immediate response.

Exercise 4.1 Stimulus-response exercise

Stimulus	Response
Cat	
Water	
Fish	
Summer	
Cold	

Is there anything that struck you while you were doing that exercise? Obviously most people's responses will not be exactly the same, although perhaps some words will initiate a very common response. This is true for situations also. We learn how to respond to events such as a fire alarm sounding, a funeral procession passing in front of us, hearing that a close friend has had a new baby, seeing our favourite sports team win or lose. It makes sense then, that if we learn, we can also unlearn, although this may be more difficult.

Why am I focusing on the idea of learning? The story of 'Lunchtime in the Staff-Room' highlights how people can respond to the same event in different ways. It is important for us to see their response as a further link in a chain that will contribute to how they respond to a similar event in the future. While an immediate anxious response may make sense, habitual anxious responses may result in a condition in its own right called anxiety. Similarly, while an immediate depressed response may make sense, habitual depressed responses may result in that condition called depression. We don't tend to see a habitual angry response as a separate condition called anger but maybe we should. We might wonder which comes first; do we react in a depressed way, because we have depression, or do we have depression because we react in a depressed way? Do we act in an anxious way because we have anxiety, or do we have anxiety because we act in an anxious way? Do we act in an angry way because we have anger, or do we have anger because we act in an angry way?

A lot has been written about the conditions of anxiety and depression but I think it is fair to say that there is still a lot of confusion, prejudice and ignorance surrounding them. The labels 'anxious' and 'depressed' can be used in a dismissive, judgemental way and can too easily become someone's identity. We need to understand the complex nature of these conditions – to understand how thoughts, feelings and actions can be automatic responses to powerful, underlying beliefs. While anxiety can lead to depression and/or anger, and depression can lead to anger and/ or anxiety, we will look at each of these conditions separately and explore how the 'Coping Triangle' and the 'Coping Sentence' can be used to help teachers who may have one or all three of these conditions relieve their stress.

Anger

It is strange to think that we label others and ourselves as 'anxious' or 'depressed' but we have no such label to describe someone who is habitually angry. To say she is 'depressed' or, my preference, 'she has depression' is very loaded and describes much more than a feeling, as we will see below. Yet, we rarely hear a fellow teacher being described as 'having anger'. The *Diagnostic and Statistical Manual of Mental Disorders* (4th edn) (DSM IV) (American Psychiatric Association, 1994) is a diagnostical tool used by clinicians to classify psychiatric difficulties. It is interesting that depression and anxiety feature as conditions, whereas anger is seen as being a feature of a condition. Let us take a few moments to explore the meaning of anger to us individually. Think of a teacher you know who has behaved in a very angry manner – see him or her as clearly as you possibly can. When did this event take place? Where was it? Where exactly were you? What were you wearing? Now complete the 'Coping Triangle' in Exercise 4.2 to establish the particular meaning that this anger had for you.

Exercise 4.2 The meaning of someone's anger for me

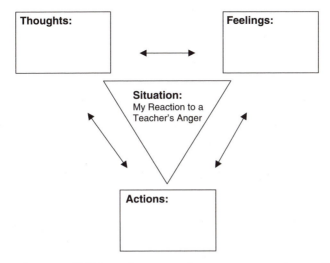

Now ask yourself if it makes sense for you to experience the feelings you have listed in the Feelings box. Did you feel scared back? Did you think, 'How dare she treat someone this way'? Did that then trigger an angry feeling? What did you do? Did you react angrily back? Did you bottle your anger up? Or did you let it go?

As we have seen, feelings generally make sense, but we can judge them, deny them or become frightened by them. Just because we feel anger does not necessarily mean that we need to respond in an angry way. This may have been our pattern up until now, but we have a choice – we can continue to respond to a stimulus that provokes us to feel angry and then react in an angry way such as lashing out verbally or physically, or we can learn to react in a different way. The 'Coping Triangle' in Figure 4.1, and reproduced below (Figure 4.4), examines the teacher Anita's anger when she walked into the staff-room and thought that her colleagues were talking about her.

Expressing thoughts, feelings and actions is the first step in the 'Coping Triangle'. The second is to examine the feelings and ask the question 'do

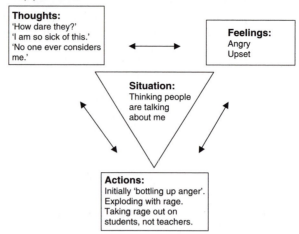

Figure 4.4 Anita's angry reaction on entering staff-room

those feelings make sense?' Given what Anita is thinking we might agree that yes, it does make sense for her to feel angry – Remember, there is nothing wrong in feeling angry, if it makes sense to do so. This is so important, as so many of us immediately blame ourselves for feeling angry, or become frightened by it and try to pretend that we actually feel calm, not angry. There is nothing wrong in feeling angry if it makes sense to do so.

The next step for Anita is encouraging her to examine her thoughts – is each thought 'helpful' or 'unhelpful'? When she thinks the thought 'How dare they?' how does she feel? – Upset and angry! When she thinks 'I am so sick of this', she automatically feels upset and angry also. Her thought 'No one ever thinks of me' is interesting and is a possible 'core belief'. If Anita really believes that no one ever thinks of her, it is understandable that she would automatically jump to immediate conclusions in all sorts of situations, which of course result in her feeling upset and angry. It might be interesting for her to explore when she began to develop her belief, but it is not necessary. Just realising that her thought is unhelpful for her might be enough. It is unhelpful for her to think that no one ever thinks of her as (a) it triggers her to feel upset and angry and (b) it might not be true that no one, no one in the whole world, ever thinks of her. It can be very tempting for us to work at convincing someone that they are wrong. In Anita's case, if she believes that no one ever thinks of her, I would be inclined to help her put in a 'maybe' – 'Maybe that is true, but maybe it is not' – rather than trying to convince her it is not so. Remember the story of the Traffic Attendants? The important thing is not whether the other teachers in the staff-room are thinking about her, but how Anita feels, thinks and acts when she believes that they are.

So, to Anita's actions: She initially 'bottles up her anger'. Understandable perhaps, but is this helpful? No. She simply is storing up her anger temporarily, for it to explode at a later time. We know from Anita's response that she took her anger out on the students in her next class. Fair? Absolutely not, but we all know teachers who do that. If we are totally honest with ourselves, we will probably admit to having taken out our anger on our students, at least once, in our teaching careers. It can be very hard when we are angry to act in a helpful, rather than an unhelpful, way. Simply put: we need to control our anger – however, that is not so simple to do. An immediate strategy for coping in a helpful way with anger is to take a deep breath, while at the same time clenching one hand into a fist – hold the breath for three seconds and then relax the hand at the same time as breathing out. This exercise works in two ways – it distracts us from immediately acting in an angry or a hurtful way and it actually does have a calming effect. The trick is to practise it over and over so that the breathing exercise, rather than an angry comment, becomes the response to certain stimuli. For instance, if a student arriving into school without his homework done is enough to 'push your buttons', it is important that you begin to associate checking students' homework with the breathing exercise. (However, as we know, it is most likely not the fact that the student has not done his homework that is bothering you most, but rather the particular meaning of that to you, which you can explore with the 'Coping Triangle'!)

Back to Anita, her angry response and possible alternative helpful actions. It is important that she acknowledges how she feels to herself and understands it, rather than blaming herself. This is where the 'Coping Sentence' comes in:

'I *feel* angry *because* I think that they are all talking about me *but maybe they are not!*'

While acknowledging our feelings of anger to ourselves is essential if we are to relieve our stress around it, it might not necessarily be wise to acknowledge it to whomever we are feeling angry with. This is because many of us tend to take things personally and so will interpret 'I am feeling angry' as 'It is your fault'. Depending on the particular meaning this has for us, we may well respond by getting angry and/or defensive ourselves.

Some years ago I misinterpreted assertive behaviour as being the same thing as aggressive behaviour and saw 'assertiveness training courses' as training people to act aggressively. That was a very misinformed and misguided view. Anita could have responded in an aggressive manner by marching over to her colleagues and demanding to know what they were talking about. Instead she chose to act in a passive-aggressive way by pretending that she was not angry or upset, but by taking it out on her students, as we have seen. She did have the option of acting in an assertive manner, which in the long run is usually much more helpful. This would have involved her acknowledging her feelings of anger to herself, accepting rather than judging them and then deciding on how she wanted to deal with this in an assertive way. This might have meant her checking out if she was correct in her assumptions about what was happening before deciding to tell the others about her upset. It might also have involved her deliberately choosing to let the reason for her anger go, rather than holding on to it. She might choose to visualise the silence or the guilty looks as a ball bouncing towards her. She can choose to pick it up and allow it to feed her anger, or she can simply choose to see it bouncing away into the nearest waste-paper basket. She might choose to deliberately open a window to let her feelings of anger out and to breathe in fresh air. Or, she might choose to leave the staff-room until she is a little calmer and then check out her interpretation of the event with someone she trusts.

'But wait,' you might ask – 'what if Anita was actually right, and her colleagues in the staff-room were talking about her? Would she not be completely correct then to just let her anger out and to tell them exactly how hurtful they are being to her?'

The answer depends on how she does this. If she chooses to respond in an angry, aggressive manner, or indeed in a passive-aggressive manner, then she is ultimately going to end up more upset. I have very deliberately used the word 'choose' in the past few sentences. Many of us do not realise that we have a choice about how to react when we are feeling angry. We do not automatically have to lash out verbally and/or physically to the person we believe is responsible for our anger (and that may well be ourselves, as well as somebody else!). Let's have another look at some possible endings for the 'Coping Sentence':

'I *feel* angry *because* I think that they are all talking about me *but I choose to act assertively!*'

'I *feel* angry *because* I think that they are all talking about me *but I choose to let it go!*'

'I *feel* angry *because* I think that they are all talking about me *but I choose not to take it personally!*'

Victims of horrific crimes such as rape and sexual abuse have spoken about the importance of their anger in helping them feel alive. Who can argue against the view that anger in such circumstances makes sense and is healthy? Yet, many victims also talk about their need, sooner or later, to let go of their anger, so as to be able to move on and live the rest of their lives free from the heavy burden of their anger. They explain that to move on and let go of their anger, they must forgive the person who has hurt them. They never describe this as an easy process – instead, it takes courage, persistence and commitment. It does not mean that they are in any way condoning or justifying the horror of what happened to them. Instead, they are very deliberately choosing not to allow it to continue destroying their present and their future lives. Those people whom I have met with who have worked to forgive those who did them harm speak of the freedom they experience when they realise that the person who hurt them no longer has the power to do so. They just will not allow that to happen any more. Perhaps the ultimate, but far from easy, 'Coping Sentence' is:

> 'I *feel* angry *because* I think that they are all talking about me *but I choose to forgive them!*'

Some teachers find it impossible to forgive – or perhaps they do not want to. There is something nice about being the victim. We can feel self-righteous about it and not want to let the other person off the hook. The only snag is, that by holding on to our anger, or our grudge, we are not letting ourselves off the hook. How many of us as students had a teacher who never forgave us, or one of our class-mates, for something that happened years before? Often I have heard teachers in staff-rooms become very heated when they resurrect old grievances and speak about them with the same intensity as if they had only just occurred. I know schools where staff relations are so bad teachers do not speak to each other, and will not even stay in the staff-room at the same time unless they absolutely have to. What benefit is to them, to their colleagues or to their students to hold on to their anger?

One of the best books I have read on Conflict Resolution is *Difficult Conversations: How to Discuss what Matters Most* by Stone *et al.* (1999). The authors assume that in any conflict situation there are two general truths: I believe I am right – you believe you are right. There is also a third way of looking at it, which may be the view of a neutral observer, such as a journalist – 'He believes he is right – you believe you are right – you are both a bit wrong and a bit right.' The authors encourage the reader to describe the conflict in terms of the 'third conversation' – i.e. how the neutral person might see it. It is a very powerful model and can indeed shift us from our sense of righteous outrage.

The feeling of anger can be a very helpful and powerful way of relieving stress. It can energise people who have formally been inert and helpless to act to change their situation for the better. I am sure Gandhi must have felt angry at times but he deliberately chose peaceful ways of dealing with this. The feeling of anger can, however, add to our sense of stress in a very real, and potentially dangerous, way. Think of Anita, who has dealt with her feelings of anger towards her colleagues by bottling them up, only to take them out on her young students later that day. She then has to face herself, and in my experience, people who are so critical and harsh on others are usually much more critical and harsh towards themselves. Anita may well experience feelings of anxiety and/or depression. These feelings may make sense, just as her feelings of anger may make sense, but left unchecked, may well turn into the conditions of anxiety and/or depression. These conditions are linked, as many people who experience one, also experience the other. Anxiety can trigger depression and depression can trigger anxiety. Anger can be a very strong feature in both, although it may be hidden and turned inwards to attack the person with the condition more than people around them. We will now turn to look at the nature of anxiety, and how the 'Coping Triangle' can help us relieve our feelings of anxiety and stress.

5   Understanding anxiety

Let us suppose that the teacher Anita reacts to thinking the other teachers are talking to her in an anxious way. As we have seen, she immediately assumes that something is wrong with her, notices herself becoming anxious and hopes that the other teachers do not notice. An hour later it is not surprising that she should react to more whispering as confirmation that there is indeed something wrong with her. What does she do? She leaves immediately to seek reassurance from the teacher next door. Reassurance does not work. It does not work because deep down she actually does believe that there is something wrong with her. She can produce countless examples to 'prove that she is right' and failing to convince her that she is wrong will be taken as further evidence that she is right! So, let us move away from trying to persuade her, or convince her that 'no, the teachers were not talking about her' and 'the students were not talking about her'. Instead, let's use the Socratic Questioning Technique to find out the particular meaning of this for her:

Anita

They are talking about me

What is so bad about that?   ⇩

I hate being talked about

What is so bad about that?   ⇩

I feel bad

What is so bad about that?   ⇩

There is something wrong with me.

If Anita begins to make the connection between her dislike of being talked about and her uncomfortable feelings, she can then begin to break or lessen the power of that connection to upset her. Feelings of anxiety are not nice – they are uncomfortable and can indeed make us feel bad. We often misinterpret the feelings of anxiety, however, with the person or incident who triggered them. The teachers in the staff-room did not cause Anita to feel anxious. Her own interpretation of the situation did!

When people begin to realise the power they have to 'make themselves anxious', they often begin to berate themselves for being 'so stupid', and can be quite harsh on themselves. Therefore, if you are noticing certain similarities between how you typically respond and Anita's anxious response, please allow yourself to be as gentle and understanding as you would automatically be towards someone else who was being overly critical of themselves!

If Anita's thought that someone is talking about her is linked with a belief that there is something wrong with her, it is understandable that she will begin to feel anxious. She may misinterpret this anxiety and view it as further evidence that there is something wrong with her rather than a normal response to a scary or worrying thought. We all do this. The example of how Ancestor Dan responds to fear in Chapter 1 illustrated the 'fight-flight' response. While we do not have to contend with real bears in our day-to-day lives we have multiple external stressors that can trigger us to produce extra adrenaline and to feel anxious: stressors at work and at home, stressors associated with leisure and stressors linked with everyday activities such as shopping. We also have internal stressors, our own thoughts, which are just as powerful in activating the 'fight-flight' response. So it really does not matter if the other teachers or students were or were not actually talking and laughing about Anita – once she thinks they were, her body responds automatically as if they were!

My way of explaining this is as follows: Let us suppose that your thoughts are the captain of a ship fuelled by coal – the captain sends a message to the men in the fire-room that there is danger ahead. They respond to this by putting more and more coal into the fire to make the ship go faster – they do not first stop and say 'Wait a minute – are you completely sure there is danger ahead? Last week you told us the same thing and it turned out that there was no danger at all, it was just your imagination.' No, they immediately and without question prepare for danger.

Our minds react in the same way. As soon as we think there is danger – we can feel scared. 'But, then,' some of you may be asking yourselves – 'why is it that I don't react to danger like that? If I think there is something dangerous I prepare myself to tackle it but do not feel terrified and unable to cope.' The difference lies in the core beliefs motoring the thoughts – the core belief 'I cannot handle being scared' will cause a very different effect than 'danger is the spice of life'!

How would I help Anita cope with her anxious response and relieve her stress? Using the 'Coping Triangle' I would help her to understand that her feelings of anxiety make sense given what she is thinking. I would then explain the nature of anxiety to her as follows:

> Anxiety is a normal reaction to something we perceive as dangerous or worrying. It is a learned response and is logical. Let us suppose that we are walking down a street, feeling perfectly calm and relaxed. A dog suddenly frightens us by barking loudly and ferociously. What happens? We *feel*: scared, nervous, sick – We *think*, 'Oh, phew, good thing that dog is locked behind the gate' and what do we *do*? We walk on. A perfectly normal response to a situation that caused us some anxiety. But look at what could happen the next time we walk down the same street:
>
> *Hearing* the same dog bark reminds us immediately of our *feelings* of fear which we experienced the first time we had the experience. Very quickly we have *thoughts* such as 'what if that gate is not secure? What if the dog got out? What if he bites me?'
>
> These scary thoughts automatically send messages to the rest of the body to prepare for danger, and so the *feelings* of fear become more intense.
>
> At this point it is understandable if we decide to play it safe and avoid the situation altogether – understandable, but not wise. For what have we learned? – To respond to a dog's barking in a very fearful way. Avoidance is not a very helpful long-term coping strategy. Using the same example we can see how walking on the other side of the road might work for a little while until we *hear* a dog barking on that side, *feel* scared and *think* that there could be a dog who might hurt us. If we continue to avoid situations we perceive as scary, we end up at home with agoraphobia – afraid to go out and with a very definite belief that we are afraid of dogs!

Some years ago Susan Jeffers wrote a book called *Feel the Fear and Do it Anyway* (Jeffers, 1989). The title is brilliant – in a nutshell it sums up the most effective way to cope with anxiety. In my experience many people would prefer to skip the first part – feeling the fear is not easy and it is much more tempting to try to block it, deny it or avoid it. I think the reason many of us do not like feeling scared is because we think it is 'stupid' – we consider our fears irrational and then we blame ourselves for being so ridiculous and/or incompetent. I have worked with children and adults who have been afraid of a wide range of things including dogs, planes, driving, stairs, lifts, spiders, giving presentations, dating, school, exams and other people. With no exception every single one of them thought they were 'stupid'. They 'knew' that their fear was irrational – they attacked themselves savagely for being so 'weak' but they also had a deep belief that they could not do whatever it was that they were afraid of. This, not surprisingly, became their reality! This would be fine if they actually felt happier as a result. They did not as their fear grew bigger and bigger and bigger.

The natural inclination of the people around them is to reassure them 'Don't worry – it is only an exam – not the end of the world.' 'You will be fine – I promise.' 'Look – everyone else can do it.' Remember: REASSURANCE DOES NOT WORK. In actual fact, it makes people who are feeling anxious feel worse. To say to someone 'It is not the end of the world' will trigger an automatic thought such as 'How do you know?' Promising that someone will be fine is equally unhelpful as we can all think of the example when the brakes failed, the rope snapped, the bomb was on board or the lift did get stuck. Reminding someone with anxiety that they are different and that everyone else can do it is probably much more unhelpful as it can trigger in them a sense of shame and reinforce their own belief that there is something wrong with them. It is natural for us to want to reassure someone – natural because it makes us feel that we are doing something to help. But it really does make the anxiety worse.

I remember working with a little girl who believed that something awful would happen to her parents if they went out in the car at night – she convinced herself that they would have an accident, be killed and that she would be left on her own. These thoughts naturally upset her and so she began to become extremely distressed at any mention that her parents might be going out any time in the future. Her reaction understandably caused her parents great distress and in their attempts to calm her they decided to reassure her that she would be safe, and that they would not go out in the car at night. What happened? Her anxiety escalated – her deep fear that something might happen to them and that she might be left alone was not addressed – in case it upset her. The truth was that it was upsetting her anyway. She continued to play scary movies in her head, which terrified her. Movies such as a neighbour calling in the middle of the night needing a lift to hospital – her parents rushing and crashing and generally the movies ended with the little girl seeing herself going to her parents' funerals. How could she not be upset when she was thinking such thoughts?

So, Anita's anxiety makes sense, given what she is thinking and what she is doing. She is asking herself if there is something wrong with her and she is seeking reassurance (see Figure 5.1).

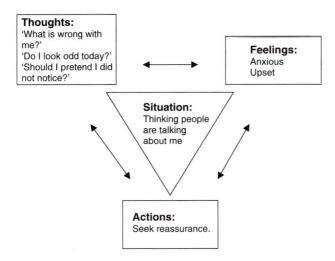

Figure 5.1 Anita's anxious response on entering the staff-room

How might Anita act in a more helpful way? You might suggest that it would be helpful for her to ask the teachers and students if they were in fact talking about her. Yes, it may be helpful, but it certainly would not be easy. Directly asking her colleagues would be similar to our ancestor facing a huge bear. Scary. Automatically, her autonomic nervous system will speed up. She will feel scared; will probably blame herself for her feelings of fear, will then worry about perhaps saying the wrong thing, or making a fool of herself, or of upsetting someone. In the short term, the easiest thing for her to do is to avoid directly facing the difficulty. The one big drawback to that is that she then reinforces that she is afraid of directly challenging situations and so her anxiety reaction will be triggered quicker and easier in the future. It is understandable that she would prefer to wait until she is feeling more relaxed. However, the nature of anxiety is that it actually increases the more we avoid facing the source of our fear. The *only* way the anxiety is going to decrease is for Anita to understand the nature of anxiety, understand that her feelings of anxiety are a natural response to what she perceives to be a difficult situation. If Anita thinks that the other teachers are talking about her and if this thought confirms her belief that there is something wrong with her, then it makes sense that she will begin to feel anxious. Focusing on her symptoms of anxiety will only make this work, so she can acknowledge how she is feeling, realise that it makes sense given how she is thinking and what she is doing and then move to use the 'Coping Sentence' to help her cope. It is important that what comes after the 'but' is strong and true as it is too easy for the critical voice in our heads to dismiss any weak ones, such as 'I feel worried about what they think of me, but it does not matter'. Of course it matters! I find the word 'maybe' very useful in reminding people like Anita that they are reacting so strongly to something that may, or may not, be true!

> 'I *feel* anxious *because* I think that they are all talking about me *but maybe they are not!*'

We now know that it is not the actual fact that people may, or may not, be talking about her which is so hurtful to Anita. Instead, it is that this thought is merely confirming her own deep, core belief that there is something wrong with her. A strong, effective 'Coping Sentence' is one that will address that belief and refute it so strongly!

> 'I *feel* anxious *because* I think that they are all talking about me *but I am more than people's opinions of me!*'

> 'I *feel* anxious *because* I think that they are all talking about me *but I choose to give them the benefit of the doubt!*'

> 'I *feel* anxious *because* I think that they are all talking about me *but I choose to believe the best of people!*'

These 'Coping Sentences' are strong and will serve to help Anita acknowledge how she is feeling, while at the same time reduce the power her feelings of anxiety and upset have over her. The more relaxed she becomes in herself, the less power she is giving to external or, more importantly, her internal thought stressors to upset her!

Before we turn to look at how to help Anita relieve her stress, if her typical way of responding is in a depressed way, I would like to highlight one final important point in coping: the role of rewards. Rewarding ourselves for progress made is actually much more difficult than we might first expect. This is so whether the reward is 'allowing' us to buy a particular CD we wanted in celebration, whether it is deliberately taking an hour to relax or whether it is giving ourselves a 'well done' pat on the shoulder. More often than not when people actually begin to face their fears and make progress they minimise their achievements and continue to focus on the dangers ahead. Or they shame themselves even more for having had the particular difficulty in the first place. We really are very harsh on ourselves.

One man I will call Robert had experienced difficulties for years in making formal public presentations at work. He had very high standards for himself and pushed himself to achieve these, regardless of the cost to his health or well-being. We explored his feelings, thoughts and actions around presentations and unearthed a very definite pattern – he believed that it was only a matter of time before he was going to make a complete mess of a presentation, with the worst thing going to happen that he would lose his job, and be seen as a failure by his entire family and friends. Therefore it is understandable that he reacted to any mention of him giving a presentation with fear – the fear then triggered more unhelpful thoughts such as 'I'm so stupid', 'Everyone else can do this so easily, what is wrong with me?', 'If they knew how hard this was for me they would never trust me again', 'What is wrong with me?', 'Why can't I pull myself together?', etc. We discovered that his habitual way of behaving was not really helpful for him, as he tended not to sleep well for nights before he was due to give a presentation; he compared himself completely unfavourably with presenters on TV as well as at work and he was obsessed about the day everyone would discover that he was a fraud.

You might expect, therefore, that Robert would have been completely thrilled when a presentation that he had been dreading for months went great. 'It went great' (his words!) not 'I made a great presentation', or 'I presented very well'. 'It went great' – as if 'it' happened, all on its own, and was nothing to do with him. I am always fascinated by our use of language – we may be absolutely certain that if the presentation had gone wrong he would have used words such as 'I fluffed/blundered/blanked/froze...' or 'I made a complete idiot of myself' or 'I am totally useless – I could not even do that presentation right'. So, perhaps it is understandable really that when he told me that 'it went great', he was not delighted and proud of himself. When I gently wondered why this was, I was met with a harsh look and words such as the following: 'Why should I congratulate myself for something which was really no big deal in the first place? It was something that everyone else could do without the drama, the fuss and the sleepless nights. Honestly, it is just pathetic that I spent so long worrying about this...'

Interesting, isn't it? We constantly berate ourselves for *not* facing our fears and yet the moment we do, we berate ourselves for not doing it quicker/easier/sooner, etc. If we think of the fearful, anxious part of ourselves as a little three-year-old child, it might make it easier to realise the huge importance of congratulating ourselves for effort and for achievement. Which of us would turn to a little child and scornfully dismiss his drawings with a sarcastic comment such as 'that house is nothing like the real thing – you need to open your eyes and look around you'. If we did we could not be surprised at the sudden refusal of the child to draw any more. It is not nice being constantly berated. In fact – it is horrible. And yet, we do it to ourselves all the time. Later we will look at how we can learn to quieten this critical voice. For the moment though it is vitally important that, despite the critical voice in our own heads, we reward ourselves for effort and for every tiny success and achievement. In fact it is good to actually write down or complete the 'Coping Triangle' if you notice that you are reacting very strongly to the idea of rewarding yourself. My suggestion is that you complete Exercise 5.1 and then have a look at Figure 5.2 and see if there are many similarities!

Exercise 5.1 *My reactions to rewarding myself*

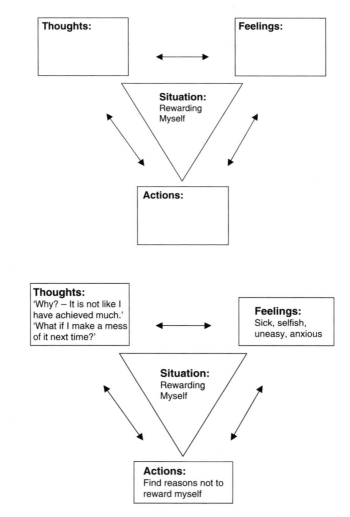

Figure 5.2 Robert's reactions to rewarding himself

You might think at first glance that Robert's feelings are over-reactions and do not make sense. But look at how he is thinking and what he is doing. Clearly there is a core-belief or two in operation here, which is sabotaging any efforts to encourage Robert to acknowledge any achievements. Let's explore this a little further using the Socratic Questioning Technique.

Robert

I have not achieved much.

What is so bad about that?   ⇓

I don't deserve to be praised.

What is so bad about that?   ⇓

I don't deserve it.

So, the bottom line for Robert is that he does not deserve praise. When he receives it externally he cringes and feels bad. When we realise that he also firmly believes that 'self-praise is no praise' we can see why the thought of actually rewarding himself for effort is so difficult for him. It is a vicious bind to be caught in – Robert puts incredible pressure on himself to perform, he immediately judges however he does as 'not good enough', dismisses any external praise or reward as 'he does not deserve it' and 'they are only being nice', begins to attack himself for not doing better and so the cycle continues. It is not surprising that he constantly feels sick, uneasy and anxious. Those feelings are a normal, logical reaction to his thoughts, beliefs and actions. The tragedy is, however, that these feelings become further evidence of just how little he deserves to be rewarded for his efforts – 'If I was presented with a reward for my presentation I would feel awful, as I would know I was a sham – I would not have deserved it and all of those people would think I did.' How is that for internal pressure? And so the cycle of anxiety, if left unchecked, will continue, resulting in sleepless nights, physical symptoms such as ulcers and migraines and probably, eventually, the ultimate self-fulfilling prophesy: poor presentations!

So what do we do? We acknowledge how we are feeling. We question and/or ignore our unhelpful thoughts and we change what we do. So, in Robert's case his 'Coping Sentence' was:

'I *feel* sick *because* I am being praised for my presentation and I do not think it was good enough, *but my inner child deserves the recognition!*'

That worked – really well and really quickly. Robert brought photos of himself as a young child into one session and we spent a long time looking at how capable, how courageous, how complete that little boy was. He then completed a 'Coping Triangle' as if he was that little boy and was upset to realise that even at that age he had judged himself so harshly.

He absolutely saw how much the little boy deserved to be recognised, to be praised and, yes, to be rewarded. He also realised that the three-year-old child had not disappeared and continued to be a part of him on a day-to-day basis.

Later we will look at concrete ways of working with the feelings of anger, anxiety and depression to help us, and the students in our care, relieve our stress. First we will turn to look at the feeling of depression and the condition of depression.

6 Understanding depression

Depression. The very word seems heavy. The word suicide seems so much heavier. These two words have become linked in recent times as many people who commit suicide have depression. At times they have become intrinsically linked and for some people the word 'depression' almost equates with the word 'suicide'. This is a very dangerous way for us to think. Everyone who has depression does not commit suicide. Everyone who commits suicide does not have depression. And yet, there is an enormous fear in society, which grows almost on a daily basis, that if someone has depression, they are in serious risk of committing suicide. We cope with this by pretending we are happy, by deliberately avoiding being unhappy and by telling ourselves and others to 'snap out of it', 'pull ourselves together' and 'be happy'. In the twenty-first century we are not allowed to be unhappy, not allowed to be miserable, not allowed to have depression. What, then, do we do with the feelings we pretend not to have?

It is vitally important that we separate out the feelings and experience of depression from the action of suicide. Later in this chapter we will look at the action of suicide, but first let us become clear on what the meaning of the word and the construct of depression is for each of us. In the past, there were very extreme views as to the causes of depression. On one side it was seen as a chemical imbalance, on the other, a complete inability to cope. Neither was particularly helpful and the true causes are much more complex and are best understood in a Bio-Psycho-Social model, i.e. people may be vulnerable towards developing depression as a result of their biological makeup and/or their psychological resources and/or their social circumstances. They may also be resilient to developing depression because of their own inner strengths, and/or external supports. Cognitive explanations for depression hold that people with depression experience a negative bias in their thoughts about the self, the world and the future (Beck, 1967). They can have absolute core beliefs such as that they are inadequate, unlovable and unacceptable and tend to think in 'black' and 'white' terms, over-generalise, ignore the positive and jump to conclusions (Burns, 1989). People with depression can experience difficulties in relating to other people and, in addition to being extremely harsh on themselves, can find it difficult to receive support from others.

Depression is a condition that responds very well to treatment – medication and/or therapy such as cognitive-behavioural therapy. Unfortunately it is increasing in severity right across the world and is now affecting people of all ages. Children, even very young children, are being diagnosed as suffering from depression. So, it is much more likely than not that as a teacher some of your colleagues will experience depression as well as some of your students. It is also not unlikely that at some time in your life, you may also experience this condition. A point to remember in reading this section is that it is not particularly experiencing depression which is most significant – rather it is the meaning of this experience for you.

Understanding the nature of depression

So let us start with the meaning for you personally. You are in your school staff-room at break and you notice that your colleague Anita is not there. When you ask you are told, 'Oh, she is on sick leave – she has depression.' What thoughts automatically whiz through your head? How do you feel and what do you do? Have a look at the responses of Teacher A and Teacher B in Table 6.1 and see whose responses resemble your own:

Table 6.1 Reponses of two teachers to hearing colleague has depression

	Thoughts	*Feelings*	*Actions*
Teacher A	'Oh, here we go again.' 'It is well for her.' 'Wouldn't we all love to stay in bed today?' 'For goodness sake would she not just pull herself together?' 'Well I hope I do not get landed with any of her class later in the day – I have my own work to do!'	Irritation Annoyance Exasperation Anger Resentment Jealousy	Express irritation in front of colleagues. Immediately voice views about not looking after her students. Question aloud as to how anyone really knows if she is ill or is just not coping.
Teacher B	'Oh, the poor thing.' 'I hope it is not too severe an attack.' 'And I thought I had problems today – at least I am able to get up and get out of the house.' 'I wonder if there is anything I can do to help?'	Sympathy Concern Worry	Express concern in front of colleagues. Immediately see if she can do anything practical to help, such as taking some extra students.

Can you imagine the tension in the staff-room between Teacher A and Teacher B? Both will feel fully justified in their response to hearing about their colleague and both will probably be convinced that they are right and that the other teacher is either 'cold, uncaring and horrible' or 'weak, gullible and stupid'. Yes, I have deliberately taken two very extreme views, but I have not exaggerated. Imagine for a moment that you are Anita, the teacher who is not able to go to school and has had to phone in sick. What might you think, feel and do? Have a look at Table 6.2.

Table 6.2 Reactions of teacher who has depression

	Thoughts	Feelings	Actions
Teacher with depression	'This is terrible.' 'I should be able to go in, but I just can't.' 'What if I feel like this tomorrow, next week, next month?' 'What will the other teachers think? – They will think I am weak, can't cope, should not be teaching.' 'What about my students?' 'What will I do if they fail their exams because of me?' 'What will I do if I meet their parents?'	Upset Overwhelmed Exhausted Hopeless Worried	Stay in bed Cry Criticise self very harshly Dwell on 'worst case scenarios'.

What have you learned about your own reactions and the meaning of depression to you? Do you feel sympathy, irritation or are you identifying more closely with the teacher who has depression? Would you automatically refer to yourself or someone else as 'depressed' or are you more inclined to say 'has depression'? You see, it is not the actual experience of depression that is significant, but the meaning of that for us – and that will be determined by a multitude of things such as our own experience with depression, and people with depression, our age, gender and life circumstances.

Do you remember how Anita thought and acted when she responded to the teachers' and students' laughter in a depressed way? (See Figure 6.1.) Can you imagine the shock many of those teachers and students might feel if they realised that Anita was actually beginning to consider suicide as a way out of her hopeless existence? They would be shocked because it is very unlikely that Anita would have confided in any of them as to how awful she really felt. Why is that? The answer may well lie with the shame and self-disgust that Anita feels towards herself and assumes that is shared by her colleagues towards her. Many people consider depression as anger turned in towards the self and in my experience, people with depression can have huge anger towards themselves for not coping to the very high (and often unrealistic) standards they set themselves.

Let's look at how Anita might respond to thinking that people are talking about her:

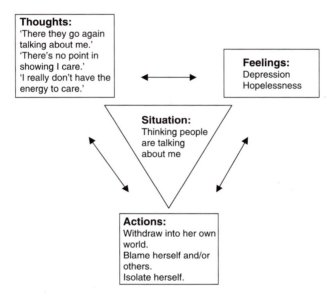

Figure 6.1 Anita's depressed response to hearing teachers and students laugh

To understand how such a tiny, relatively insignificant event as thinking people are talking about her might be a catalyst for Anita in triggering suicidal thoughts, let us see how her story might develop when later that same day she walked into the staff-room and noticed her colleagues' sudden silence.

Immediately following her last class that day Anita went home, collapsed in front of the television and sat there for two hours. She later got up and, as she was too tired to cook, phoned for a take-away meal to be delivered. She made some attempt to tidy the kitchen but was overwhelmed by her feelings of tiredness. Her heart sank as she heard the key turn in the front door and realised that her flatmate had met the deliveryman on the doorstep. She tried to squash her feelings of guilt and shame that she was having another convenience meal and instead deliberately tried to lighten her voice and look alert and interested.

When asked about how her day had gone she lied and said it was 'fine' before immediately changing the subject. She did not consider confiding in her for one moment – how could she admit that she had 'over-reacted' so badly? She picked at her meal instead and forced herself to seem interested in what her flatmate was saying. The effort became too much and she reverted to silence, resenting her various attempts to involve her. It was a relief really when finally her flatmate lost her patience and stormed into a different room, leaving Anita to wonder, yet again, why her flatmate stayed with her, and if she would actually notice if she did move out.

Forcing herself to clean the kitchen she then went to bed, realising how totally exhausted she was and hoping that for at least once this week she would sleep until the clock woke her. But, no, once again she woke at four-thirty am, and lay there unable to get back to sleep. She considered her life, and compared the reality of it with her dreams and plans.

So, there it is – the lonely, horrible struggle of a teacher with depression, who is crucifying herself for not meeting her own impossible standards and who is not asking for and not accepting any form of social support. You might wonder why she does not just go to the doctor and get some help there. Well, let us suppose that she finally does, as she realises that she cannot keep going much longer with so little sleep. What happens?

Anita finally visits her doctor and explains that she has been having difficulties in sleeping, as she continually wakes up early in the mornings and then cannot get back to sleep again. Her appetite has decreased and she has lost weight. She is worried that her energy levels have dropped considerably and has noticed that her concentration and ability to focus were also not as good as they had been. The doctor asks her if she has been under a lot of stress recently and Anita shrugs and says 'a bit'. The doctor then concludes that she 'is depressed' and prescribes anti-depressant medication.

'Great,' we might think. Now, she will be sorted – she has an illness and provided she takes her medication as prescribed she will be back to normal very soon. That is not necessarily so. We must be very careful not to underestimate the power of the 'depression' label to actually increase, rather than relieve, stress. For some people the diagnosis of depression is a relief – it can mean that they are not going mad, but instead have a medically recognised illness that can be treated with medication – wonderful. These people take their tablets diligently and notice with relief any sign that they are getting better. This is not the case with Anita, however, as we can see in Figure 6.2.

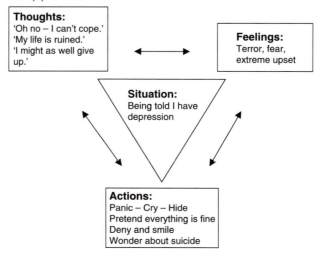

Figure 6.2 The meaning of depression to Anita

Obviously Anita's reaction to being told that she had depression was very severe and she immediately described herself as 'being depressed'. Let's use the Socratic Questioning Technique to explore the meaning of this for her.

Anita's responses made absolute sense to her. As a very young child she had witnessed her mother not being well due to depression. For years she was vigilant in reminding her to take her tablets, as she believed that they would make her better. She coped by denying and smiling. Denying that she was worried about her mother and denying that anything was wrong at home. She smiled – constantly – and was never sad, never upset and never, ever in need of sympathy. As she grew up she became determined never, ever to take medication and to never admit that there was anything wrong.

Anita's story is fictitious, but it is very true to the experience of many, many people. So, not surprisingly, when a GP who does not know the meaning of the label for people such as Anita tells them that they are depressed and need medication, they see themselves as failures.

So what can Anita do? Let's see how the 'Coping Triangle' can help her make sense of her distress and help relieve pressure:

> It is not surprising to discover that Anita is extremely critical and harsh towards herself. She monitors everything she does – big and small – to ensure that she has not failed in anything (big or small) and, particularly, to ensure that she is always happy. Let us suppose that in the previous six months before she attended her GP Anita had been unsuccessful in her bid for promotion within her school. A relationship that had begun very well had ended suddenly and three of her students had failed in her subject in their state exams. Anita's responses to the 'Coping Triangle' are presented in Table 6.3.

Do you notice a pattern? The first step in the 'Coping Triangle' is to identify the feelings, thoughts and actions connected to a particular event. The second is to ask the question 'Do these feelings make sense?' What do you think? Do Anita's feelings of embarrassment, feeling stupid and anger at herself make sense? Notice what is in your head as you wonder about this. Do you feel that she is justified in feeling this way or do you feel that these feelings are unwarranted, unnecessary, or just wrong? Pay close attention to this, as this will give you valuable information as to how tolerant and accepting you are of your own feelings! So, do Anita's feelings make sense? Given what she is thinking, I would say that they make absolute sense. Consider for a moment that Anita was directing all her thoughts, not at herself, but at a little three-year-old child. We would probably expect that the little one would instantly believe that all the criticisms were warranted and that, in fact, there was something definitely wrong with her. Therefore it would not be surprising for her to feel embarrassed, shamed and upset and become self-critical and angry.

So, yes, given how harshly Anita is treating herself, I would say that her feelings make perfect sense. Therefore, we then move on to consider the third and fourth steps of the 'Coping Triangle': Are her thoughts and her actions helpful or unhelpful? Again, I ask you to have a look at these and then place a mark in either the helpful or unhelpful column in Exercises 6.1 and 6.2.

Table 6.3 Anita's reactions to recent events

	Thoughts	Feelings	Actions
Unsuccessful in bid for promotion	'Why did I bother?' 'Everyone pities me.' 'What is wrong with me that I did not get it?' 'There is no future for me in this school.' 'I should not have bothered.' 'I am close to giving up.' 'What is wrong with me?'	Embarrassed Shamed Upset Feels stupid Angry at self	Constantly question herself as to where she went wrong. Continually replay interview in her head. Criticise herself relentlessly for not doing better. Deny in public that she was upset or bothered at not getting it. Pretend that she was fine.
End of relationship	'I am a disaster at relationships.' 'What did I do this time?' 'I thought this was going to be it – why did I go and ruin it?' 'Why did I tell everyone?' 'I was pathetic and silly to be happy so soon.' 'I was stupid and ridiculous.' 'When will I grow up?' 'What is wrong with me?'	Embarrassed Shamed Upset Feels stupid Angry at self	Constantly question herself as to where she went wrong. Continually replay events of relationship in her head. Criticise herself relentlessly for not having made it work. Deny in public that she was upset or bothered at the relationship ending. Pretend that she was fine.
Failure of three students in state exams	'I let them down.' 'I should have known that they were not working hard enough.' 'I have ruined their chances of a good career.' 'That is what I get for being so smug about my teaching abilities.' 'Pride comes before a fall.' 'What is wrong with me?'	Embarrassed Shamed Upset Feels stupid Angry at self	Constantly question herself as to where she went wrong. Continually replay events in various classes in her head. Criticise herself relentlessly for not having worked harder. Deny in public that she was upset or bothered at her students not passing. Pretend that she was fine.

Exercise 6.1 How I describe Anita's thoughts about recent events

	Anita's thoughts	Helpful	Unhelpful
Unsuccessful in bid for promotion	'Why did I bother?' 'Everyone pities me.' 'What is wrong with me that I did not get it?' 'There is no future for me in this school.' 'I should not have bothered.' 'I am close to giving up.' 'What is wrong with me?'		
End of relationship	'I am a disaster at relationships.' 'What did I do this time?' 'I thought this was going to be it – why did I go and ruin it?' 'Why could I not play it cool?' 'Why did I tell everyone?' 'I was pathetic and silly to be happy so soon.' 'I was stupid and ridiculous.' 'When will I grow up?' 'What is wrong with me?'		
Failure of three students in state exams	'I let them down.' 'I should have known that they were not working hard enough.' 'I have ruined their chances of a good career.' 'That is what I get for being so smug about my teaching abilities.' 'Pride comes before a fall.' 'What is wrong with me?'		

Exercise 6.2 How I describe Anita's actions to recent events

	Anita's actions	Helpful	Unhelpful
Unsuccessful in bid for promotion	Constantly question herself as to where she went wrong. Continually replay interview in her head. Deny in public that she was upset or bothered at not getting it. Pretend that she was fine.		
End of relationship	Constantly question herself as to where she went wrong. Continually replay events of relationship in her head. Criticise herself relentlessly for not having made it work. Deny in public that she was upset or bothered at the relationship not developing. Pretend that she was fine.		
Failure of three students in state exams	Constantly question herself as to where she went wrong. Continually replay events of certain classes in her head. Criticise herself relentlessly for not having worked harder. Deny in public that she was upset or bothered by her students not passing. Pretend that she was fine.		

Well, how did you get on with that exercise? Did you notice that Anita has some very definite patterns in how she thinks and how she acts? She is without doubt extremely self-critical of herself and it would not be too much of an exaggeration to say that she has a 'Self-Critic Monster' inside her that she is continually feeding by her habit of playing back events in her past she is not pleased with. Over, and over and over. Remember how light is the usual, automatic response to pressing a light switch, water to the tap being turned on and fear to us having a scary thought? It is also true that if we think self-critical thoughts in a harsh, judgemental, angry way, we are going to feel shame and upset.

It is not surprising therefore that Anita developed depression. Let us reflect on what we know of Anita – she has spent years of her life pretending to herself and to the world that she is always happy. She has decided at a very young age that she will always cope and will never, ever be like her mother. She becomes a teacher – a very good one, who has high standards and high expectations of her students as well as of herself. Mostly she copes and is seen by the other teachers as 'easy-going', 'happy' and 'always in good form'. Not surprisingly, her body begins to object to her refusal to acknowledge that there is anything wrong and that actually she is engaged in a constant savage inner attack as well as experiencing difficulties in her work and personal life. Not surprisingly she begins to have difficulties in sleeping, in concentrating and notices that she has low energy.

It is not surprising either that Anita reacts so strongly against being told by her GP that she has depression, or in Anita's words 'she is depressed'. Let's recap on steps one to four of the 'Coping Triangle' as a way of helping her to cope with her depression.

Step 1:	Identify Anita's feelings, thoughts and actions.	
Step 2:	Do Anita's feelings make sense?	Yes
Step 3:	Are Anita's thoughts helpful or unhelpful?	All unhelpful
Step 4:	Are Anita's actions helpful or unhelpful?	All unhelpful

Step 5 involves helping Anita become aware of her underlying core beliefs. Based on what we know about her these may be along the lines of:

- If I get depression I am a failure
- I must always be happy
- I must never, ever admit to being unhappy

We can help Anita understand that the power of her beliefs lie in the fact that she believes them!

Step 6 is the final step and brings Anita's feelings, thoughts and actions together in the 'Coping Sentence'. We could explore several possibilities, such as *'but I am learning to respect my feelings'* and *'but that is OK because I am allowed to feel upset'*. My guess is that the one that will make the most impact on her and seems to be the most powerful is *'but I choose to acknowledge my feelings and I choose to act in a helpful way'*.

> 'I *feel* upset, shamed and embarrassed *because* I did not get promotion *but I choose to acknowledge my feelings and I choose to act in a helpful way.'*
>
> 'I *feel* upset, shamed and embarrassed *because* my relationship did not work out *but I choose to acknowledge my feelings and I choose to act in a helpful way.'*
>
> 'I *feel* upset, shamed and embarrassed *because* three of my students failed their exams *but I choose to acknowledge my feelings and I choose to act in a helpful way.'*
>
> 'I *feel* sick, worried and frightened *because* I have depression *but I choose to acknowledge my feelings and I choose to act in a helpful way.'*

There is no doubt that acknowledging her feelings will be difficult for Anita. Years of pretending, denying and bottling up feelings will have made her so wary and judgemental of her tears, her sadness, and of her anger. When she reminds herself that she chooses to act in a helpful way, it focuses her on her actions. She realises that berating herself continually because she did not get the job is unhelpful and is bemused to discover how little she actually knows about how to help herself act in a more helpful way. She discovers that the words 'I choose' become very powerful for her. She chooses to attend a GP for a medical opinion on her health. She chooses to take any prescribed medication as advised by her GP. She chooses to ring a friend and go to the cinema. She then chooses to tell the same friend later about her upset when her relationship ended. She chooses to talk to her students about how much responsibility she was taking over their exams and to formally hand that responsibility back to them. She chooses to engage in professional therapy to become aware of her own feelings towards herself, her mother and depression.

So far in this book we have focused on teachers' experiences of anger, anxiety and depression. It is natural that our students will also feel angry, feel anxious and feel depressed. How many of us allow or tolerate such feelings in our classrooms? Our reactions to how students express their feelings of anger, anxiety and depression may exacerbate the situation. Yes, we can legitimately *feel* angry because a particular student will not sit down, keep quiet and do his work. We cannot legitimately, or indeed, morally, act on our anger in a way that is harmful to that student. Most of us know that we cannot physically attack a student, but how many of us in our teaching careers can raise our hands high and say in truth that we have never verbally attacked a student? Oh, we might feel completely justified – that student may have provoked us so many times that one day he just went too far, we might tell ourselves that our sarcastic comment was mild, compared with what we would have liked to have said. We might convince ourselves that good discipline requires us to show our 'smart alec' students 'who is boss'. We might think all of these things, and indeed we might believe them too, but just as most people in the world now acknowledge that the belief that the world is flat is untrue, we would be wrong. It is never right for us as teachers to act in a way that is harmful to the students in our care.

So, what do we do when our students provoke us to such an extent? We must first of all accept personal responsibility for allowing ourselves to be provoked in the first place. The calmer and more relaxed we are, the better we are able to separate out our students' feelings of anger, anxiety and depression from our own. The calmer and more relaxed we are, the better we are able to act and react in a responsible manner to our students' feelings of anger, anxiety and depression. The key secret to stress relief for teachers is *RELAX.*

'Relax? RELAX?' I can almost hear the shouts of the many angry, frustrated teachers who may chance upon this book. 'How can I be relaxed when Mary Smith insists on back answering me every time I have the misery of teaching her?' 'How can I be relaxed when I know the state exams are three weeks away, I know the students do not know what I have taught them and I know that I have at least half of the programme left to cover?' 'How can I be relaxed when the parents of my students hold me responsible for my students' grades?' 'How can I relax when the Principal has warned me that he does not want to hear so much noise coming from my classroom?' 'How can I relax when I have children who are not able to learn seeking my attention, and children who do not want to learn seeking everyone else's attention?'

I never said teaching was an easy job. In my experience it is not. While it continues to be an immensely rewarding job, I have found it to be frustrating, difficult, exhausting and at times demoralising. I have had moments in my teaching career to date where my inner critic has screamed at me for treating children in such a harsh, demanding way. The same critic has, on other occasions, screamed at me for being too soft and too easy. I have felt ashamed at how harsh I was towards a particular child, guilty at having spoken to a child in a way I would hate being spoken to myself and angry at myself for not coping better. It is a definite truth, however, that the less relaxed I am the more I experience these feelings and situations. The more relaxed I am, the better I am able to acknowledge my own feelings, accept them and deal with them in a way which is respectful and kind to myself as well as respectful and kind to the students in my care.

Yes, the secret to stress relief is really RELAX! How? So far in this chapter we have looked at the feelings and thoughts parts of the 'Coping Triangle'. Later we will turn to focus on how we can increase our range and our ability to use helpful, rather than unhelpful, actions in the course of our teaching. First, however, I would like us to consider the most unhelpful action available to us as adults, as well as to the students in our care: suicide.

Suicide

The increase in suicide in the Western world is horrific and frightening. The reality is that even very young children now see it as an 'option' as something available for them to do. Although the lyrics of a particular song hold that 'suicide is painless', many of us know that is not true. Many of us, but not all. Remember the discussion on the power of beliefs? Many people who attempt or succeed at suicide genuinely believe that the world would be much better without them, or they believe that the pain of continuing to live in the world is so much more difficult than the pain of ending their own lives. Lots of myths prevail about suicide, which we now know are not in fact true. One is 'if he talks about it, he'll never do it'. Not true. Another is 'if you talk about it, you'll only put the idea into his head'. Not true. A third is 'if he attempts it once, he will keep on doing it until he succeeds'. Also not true. The terrible tragic thing is, though, that many, many young people do not know that these myths are not true. They believe that because they have the thought 'My family would be better off if I was dead', they are suicidal and become frightened by, and yet obsessed with, their suicidal thoughts. It is crucial that they are helped to separate out thoughts from actions. Just because I am thinking I would like a biscuit, a drink, or to end my own life, does not mean that I actually have to go and do it. Yet having a suicidal thought can be genuinely terrifying. The terror can then generate more thoughts such as 'I am going mad' or 'I am such a burden on my family and friends', which can then lead to obsessing about 'how to do it'.

A few years ago I asked the twenty-five student teachers in my tutorial group how many of them had personally known someone who died by suicide. A staggering twenty-three of them had. Too many people now see suicide as an option. This raises an important question for us as teachers. How vigilant must we be about acting if we think a colleague is suicidal? How vigilant must we be if we think that a child in our class is suicidal? How might we know? And how can we actively work to prevent suicide? The answers to these are addressed in the next chapter: Coping with anger, anxiety and/or depression in the classroom.

7 Coping with anger, anxiety and/or depression in the classroom

Feelings of anger, anxiety and depression left unchecked can multiply and spread. There are times in the school year when it makes absolute sense that teachers and students will experience one or all of these feelings. The start of the new school year and the period coming up to exams can be very exciting, very challenging or very scary. Some people experience events as all three, and relish the challenge; others focus on their own internal response to fear, and hence, normal anxiety can become a problem. So what can we do? We can become aware of our feelings and thoughts and we can choose to act on them in a helpful, responsible way. We need to be aware of key aspects of the nature of the conditions of anxiety and depression, which are expanded on below. Finally we need to become aware of helpful actions we can take in helping ourselves, our colleagues and our students cope with the feelings of anger, anxiety and depression.

Key aspects of the nature of anxiety

1 The anxiety response is a normal, logical response to perceived internal or external threat.
2 It is not the event, but the meaning of the event, which causes the distress.
3 The meaning varies according to an individual's age, experience, beliefs and fears.
4 Teachers may never know the true meaning of an event to their student.
5 Feelings of anger, anxiety and/or depression can spread to others and if unchecked can increase in frequency and intensity.
6 The more aware and relaxed teachers are about their own response to anger, anxiety and depression, the better able they will be to help the students in their class cope.
7 Reassurance does not work and can actually serve to increase the level of anxiety experienced.

Let's look at these points in a little more detail:

The anxiety response is a normal, logical response to perceived internal or external threat We may under-estimate just how many opportunities there can be in a classroom for perceived internal or external threat. From a teacher's point of view external threats might come in the form of her own health; students; other teachers; the curriculum; parents; school management; inspectors; inadequate space, heating or lighting; noise; poor teaching materials and resources. Internal threats may be triggered by an actual external threat but are mainly due to teachers' own anxious interpretations of internal or external events. Unhelpful cognitions that may trigger the anxiety response include the following:

- 'What will I do if the teacher next door complains about all the noise in the classroom?'
- 'I just can't seem to get it through to this class that they have to do some work.'
- 'Oh, no, the School Principal is at the door – what have I done?'
- 'The exams are in a few weeks and I still have not finished the course – if the class do not do well, it is going to be my fault.'
- 'I hope the students do not realise that I do not know much about this subject.'

Students' external threats vary but can include their own health; their performance in the classroom; other students in the classroom (those they like as well as those they dislike!); the teacher; school management; parents; the physical environment of the classroom; the subject. As with teachers, internal threats may be triggered by their own cognition to external circumstances. Some examples of students' anxiety triggering thoughts are:

- 'What if Amanda realises I like her?'
- 'What if Amanda thinks I don't like her?'
- 'What if the gang think I like Amanda?'
- 'What if Amanda likes me?'
- 'What if Amanda doesn't like me?'
- 'What if Amanda likes Adrian Murray?'

It is not the event, but the meaning of the event, which causes the distress To illustrate this point think again of yourself, aged fifteen, walking into the corridor of your Secondary school. A group of your class-mates are at the opposite end of the hall laughing loudly. As you walk in, they suddenly stop and look at you. What is likely to be your automatic thought? Practically all of us will automatically assume that they have been talking about us. But we will have very different reactions depending on the particular meaning of that event to us. For instance we may:

- Think that they were talking about us, feel ashamed and sneak away quietly.
- Think that they were talking about us, feel angry and confront them aggressively.
- Think that they were talking about us, feel delighted and assume that they were at the match and saw us score all of those goals for the team.

In each case, it is the same event, the same assumption, but completely different meanings with different conclusions.

The meaning varies according to an individual's age, experience, beliefs and fears   This is evident throughout this chapter. In the last example the student who sneaks away quietly may be younger, less confident, have experience in the past of being talked about and bullied and may believe that nobody really likes him anyway. The student who reacts angrily may have learned to respond to such events in an aggressive, rather than an anxious, manner. He may believe that nobody has the right to discuss him ever. The student who has the delighted reaction may have completely misinterpreted the situation, but if he believes that he is surrounded by people who are interested and delighted in his successes, it is understandable why he might jump to the particular conclusion he did!

Teachers may never know the true meaning of an event to their student   That is one of these simple truths that we can easily dismiss. We may never, ever know how a student really reacts to us – our remark to another teacher in a school corridor that we 'did not really expect any better' from a particular student might trigger a student to give up trying in the classroom and we may never know that he did not overhear the rest of the sentence 'but he really surprised me, as well as himself, by his efforts'. Another example to illustrate this point is how my reaction to a particular sports event compared with a friend's reaction. I was delighted that the winner had the composure, skill and luck to finally win a particular competition. My friend glumly announced that he had bet on the other person to win and as a result did not share my delight! Same event, different meaning!

Feelings of anger, anxiety and/or depression can spread to others and if unchecked can increase in frequency and intensity   Some years ago I was studying a course in university that did not have exams at the end of one academic year. With a week or so to go before exams were due to start for the rest of the university, I decided that I would really enjoy wandering through the library. It is a pity that there were not 'before and after' photographs taken to illustrate how quickly I transformed from a calm, relaxed, content person into a jittery, anxious, upset one. On my stroll through a small section of the library I literally absorbed the anxiety that was existent in almost everyone else. My leisurely stroll was very short and I did not return to the library again until all of the exams were well over and the general atmosphere had returned to normal. There is a reason why we are told not to panic in certain situations, such as a fire in a cinema. Tragically there are countless examples right across the world where people did not follow this direction and innocent people were crushed to death.

Generally in a classroom we are not talking about life and death, although if the fire alarm goes it is of course vital that the students do not panic. But have you ever noticed how one class can be so much more anxious about exams than another? It is as if the anxiety has become a permanent fixture in the classroom. It is also true that children look to adults as well as to their peers for their cues. If you, the teacher, are very anxious, for whatever reason, you may be guaranteed that some children in the class will also become anxious. This leads us directly on to the next point.

The more aware and relaxed teachers are about their own response to anger, anxiety and depression, the better able they will be to help the students in their class cope Occasionally people misinterpret 'relaxed' as meaning 'easy-going' and 'easy-going' as meaning 'careless'. A 'good' teacher may be seen as the one who WORRIES about her students, and about how they will perform in exams and who goes out of her way to make them as prepared as possible. Teachers and parents may fall into the trap of excessive anxiety over the students' performance to the point where they actually end up doing their work for them. The students will pick up on the anxiety but not learn the skills to cope with this.

When a teacher is aware of her own anxiety and is relaxed about this she is less likely to project her fears onto her students. Instead she can acknowledge her fears, make sense of them, take responsibility for them and do something proactive to cope. Her 'Coping Sentence' might be as follows: 'I feel anxious because the exams are coming up next week and I do not think some of the students are going to do well, *but I cannot do the exam for them.*' This may well have the effect of placing appropriate responsibility onto the students, which is not a bad idea!

Reassurance does not work and can actually serve to increase the level of anxiety experienced No matter how many times I see the truth of this I still find myself wanting to reassure parents, teachers and students who are anxious. It is natural, but unhelpful. Just imagine that you are leaving your home to go on a journey. You are in a rush and go through the motions of leaving on automatic pilot until you find yourself in the car ready to leave. Just as you are about to start the car a thought pops into your head: 'Did I lock the front door?' – the natural thing at that point is for us to jump back out of the car and check – yes, reassurance at that level works and is helpful. But, what if we get back into the car and then question ourselves again: 'Did I really check it properly?' This is tricky as most of us would again get out and check it again. If the same thing happens a third time our reassuring ourselves that the door is locked through checking is no longer helpful. At this point we may get another person to check for us, and for a time we will believe them and will be reassured – for a time. Annoying, anxious thoughts will inevitably pop straight back in: 'But did he really check it properly? I don't know, maybe I should ask someone else ...' And so the pattern goes on, logically, but with a rapidly increasing level of anxiety. No, reassurance does not work and may in fact exacerbate feelings of anxiety.

Helpful actions in coping with anxiety

Knowledge can actually make things worse, as it can add fuel to our harsh, critical voices. When we become aware of the consequences of unhelpful actions such as avoidance, horrible sarcastic taunts enter our head. Taunts such as 'See, you know this is the wrong thing to do, but you have to do it anyway – Coward!' Obviously, these can be very difficult to deal with and are extremely unhelpful as, unchecked, they can make us feel worse, and may even contribute to us developing depression as well as anxiety. Therefore it is absolutely vital that we take action that is helpful and that we do so in as gentle a way as possible. The better we are at understanding and coping with our own anxiety, the better we will be able to help the students in our care. The possible actions that are listed below are suggestions and can be adapted to suit particular situations.

Helpful actions in coping with anxiety include

1   Accept that the anxiety response is a normal and logical response to perceived internal or external threat.
2   Determine the meaning of the anxiety for you and/or your students.
3   Contain the anxiety as much as possible.
4   Focus on deliberately breathing slowly.
5   Ignore unhelpful thoughts through distraction.
6   Repeat a strong 'Coping Sentence' frequently.
7   Limit intake of caffeine and sugar.
8   Obtain helpful support if appropriate to do so.
9   Break large tasks down into achievable tasks.
10   Encourage and reward for effort as well as for success.

Accept that the anxiety response is a normal and logical response to perceived internal or external threat   This might be easier said than done at first, but is a vital first step. As we have seen, many people who experience anxiety see their reactions as a sign of weakness or 'stupidity' and are very harsh on themselves as a result. If we can see the anxiety response in terms of the coalmen in a huge ocean liner, we will begin to appreciate that it is only 'following orders'. That frees us from blaming the coalmen and focusing on who is responsible – the captain – in this case our thoughts and our beliefs. Accepting the anxiety response can be freeing and can break the critical judgemental pattern. The first part of the 'Coping Sentence' is important; 'I feel _____ because _____'. This allows us to feel the anxiety and to link it with something that makes sense. Anxiety always makes sense – it may be that our perception of the perceived internal or external threat is wrong, but that is not the anxiety response's fault! To blame ourselves for being stupid because we feel anxious when we have just triggered that response is as unfair and as unhelpful as the captain of that ocean liner blaming his coalmen for making the ship go faster – they did just what he told them!

Determine the meaning of the anxiety for you and/or your students   This is important. We cannot assume that the meaning of anything is the same for others as it is for us. We saw in Chapter 1 how three people might share the same worry of having an accident, but that the meaning if they did have an accident is very different. We may consider a child in our class to be ridiculous, tiresome and totally over-reacting when he is upset at 'only' getting 90 per cent in an exam instead of 95 per cent. Instead of dismissing him, ridiculing him, or reassuring him, we need to explore gently with him what exactly the meaning of his grade is to him. One very effective way of doing this is to ask: 'What is so bad about only getting 90 per cent?' Depending on his response, we may have to follow the line of Socratic questioning a little, but we will generally find that his upset is due to either a particular thought or belief he has. Perhaps he is determined to do better in exams than an older sibling, perhaps he believes that he is exceptionally bright and that anything less than 95 per cent is the same as failure, or perhaps ... There are endless possibilities, but rather than assuming, we need to explore the specific meaning with the student. Then we can help him see how his anxiety response is a normal, logical reaction to events, or his interpretation of events.

Contain the anxiety as much as possible   Human nature is intriguing. If I asked you at this moment not to think of a snowman with a carrot for his nose, it would practically be impossible not to. Almost instantaneously, a picture of a snowman with a carrot for his nose will suddenly pop into our heads. So, if I say to you 'don't worry' it almost guarantees that some part of your brain will begin to initiate the 'worry process'. Many scriptwriters have capitalised on the 'Don't Panic' announcements on planes, creating some hilarious movies in the process. It is almost as if we are sitting there, quite relaxed and suddenly when we hear 'don't panic' we have automatic thoughts such as 'Why? What is there to panic about – should I be panicking? Why is everyone else panicking? Do they know something I do not know?' Within a class environment it does make sense that students will worry if they are faced with an exam. Allowing them to feel that worry is actually a much more helpful action than telling them not to worry!

Focus on deliberately breathing slowly   Breathing slowly is a very important helpful action for two reasons. First of all it actually can calm us down, and secondly it distracts ourselves from unhelpful thoughts and actions by focusing us on something productive. The simple exercise of breathing in while at the same time clenching the left fist, holding the breath for three seconds and then breathing out through the mouth, while at the same time relaxing the hand works! Naturally, the more often it is practised when it is not needed, the better and quicker it will work when it is. I encourage people to practise that exercise in rounds of three, many times during the day. It is as if they are creating a reservoir of relaxation that will be there for when they need it.

Breathing slowly is central to meditation, yoga, tai-chi and countless relaxation exercises. The value of learning and incorporating such exercises into our daily lives cannot be emphasised enough.

Ignore unhelpful thoughts through distraction   I wonder what thought went through your head when you read the suggestion of learning and practising relaxation exercises? Was it something like 'Oh, I know I should do that, but I never have time' or 'I tried that and hated it'? As we saw in the first chapter, thoughts can be automatic, unhelpful and untrue. It is very difficult, if not impossible, to stop thinking a particular thought, and really the more we focus on 'not thinking' it, the more difficult it can be not to. The good news is that distraction works – it really does. Distraction breaks the connection between the thought and the feeling, or between the thought and the action. For instance, I might have the thought 'Oh, today is the day my friend is going for the results of her medical tests'. Automatically I could begin to think some very scary thoughts such as 'What if the news is bad?'. 'She doesn't deserve this to happen to her.' 'It is not fair.' 'I hope she won't have to have chemotherapy.' 'She will hate to lose her hair.' 'What if . . .' 'What if . . .' and 'What if . . .' There would be something wrong with me if I did not begin to feel upset and anxious as a result of my thinking. The easiest way to help myself cope with my anxiety is not to indulge in thinking all those thoughts in the first place. Yes, certainly the first one might pop into our heads unannounced and unwanted, but we do not have to go down the 'what if' path. My very wise and much loved Aunty Noreen used to say 'I have no room in my head for that'. We can choose to distract ourselves from our thoughts just as we can choose to close our eyes to something scary on TV. We can distract ourselves through actions such as cleaning out the fridge. We can also distract ourselves with the 'Coping Sentence'.

Repeat a strong 'Coping Sentence' frequently Let's look again at the thought 'Oh, today is the day my friend is going for the results of her tests'. Instead of allowing ourselves to go down the line of unhelpful thoughts we can use the 'Coping Sentence' as follows: 'I feel worried because my friend is getting her results today (that makes sense!) *but I choose to distract myself until I hear from her.*'

The following 'Coping Sentence' works well with people who are anxious: 'I feel _____ because _____ *but distraction works.*' The focus is then put on how they might distract themselves. Sometimes people prepare themselves in advance with index cards on which they have written prompts such as 'My favourite film/book/song is . . .' 'A lovely place to go on holiday to is . . .' 'When I have finished this course I am going to . . .' I also encourage people to distract themselves by guessing how many triangles they can see around them and then counting to see how close they were to being right! This idea serves to distract them while at the same time reminding them of the 'Coping Triangle'. Try it yourself, just now. How many triangles do you think you will see around you? Spend a few moments counting them. Once you begin to realise that corners of rooms and doors are in the shape of triangles you will realise that there probably are a lot more than you had initially realised.

If you have a strong religious and/or spiritual sense you might like to complete the 'Coping Sentence' with a prayer such as '*but I trust in God, Yahweh, a Higher Power*', or even '*but I choose to trust*'. It is important never to impose your own 'Coping Sentence' on to any one else, as they are so individual. When you have one that works well for you, then you need to create opportunities to remind yourself to use it! Write it on pieces of paper and keep them in various bags and pockets. You might prefer to use a code such as 'BITIG' (but I trust in God); you can then freely write on the back of your hand! It can be a great idea to associate your 'Coping Sentence' with an object – again, it could be a triangle, or maybe a green traffic light, or a rain cloud. It does not really matter what, so long as it is something that will remind you to identify how you are feeling, link it to something that makes sense and then do something helpful to help you cope!

Limit intake of caffeine and sugar Talking about 'doing something helpful'!!! A few years ago I went to a lecture given by Professor Jack James who is a psychologist who has spent many years researching the short-term and long-term effects of caffeine on people. His findings were so convincing that not only did I completely give up drinking coffee, I also gave up taking a particular migraine medication which contained caffeine. I was not prepared for the extreme migraine I experienced as a result – it lasted a week and was so severe that my family begged me to take the medication. While I still get migraine, it is neither as severe nor as frequent as when I was taking the caffeine. I have discovered that Professor James was correct when he said that once we give up drinking coffee we realise that we do not even like it!

What are your own personal beliefs about caffeine? Are you convinced that you cannot function until you have your first cup of coffee in the day? Caffeine is definitely a stimulant and even if you do not want to give it up totally, it is a very good idea to curtail your intake of it when you are particularly anxious. Believe me, caffeine does not help. If you want evidence of this I would encourage you to read some of Professor James's research such as James and Gregg (2004a, 2004b). A list of his most recent research papers can be found in the Department of Psychology website of the National University of Ireland Galway (http://www.nuigalway.ie/psy/stf_jj.html).

Sugar? I would love to be able to say that I have successfully given up sugar too. Unfortunately I have not, but in the past three years I have become aware of how dependent I am on sugar and how it affects me, particularly during times of pressure. I have a strong suspicion that my migraine is linked with my intake of sugar, but as I wrote earlier, knowledge on its own is not enough – my own particular 'Coping Sentence' for this is 'I feel guilty because I am eating too much sugar *but I have a choice*'. This has the powerful and immediate effect of changing me from 'automatic pilot' to seriously deciding if I want to choose to eat the sugary temptation. So what is so bad about sugar? Have you noticed how young children react if they have just had sugary drinks and lots of sweet bars? They can transform rapidly into something resembling hyperactive little monsters. The part which the manufacturers love is that sugar is addictive – the more we get, the more we want, and if we are deprived it, we crave it. It is a very difficult cycle to break out of. It is imperative that we do however. The rate of diabetes among children and adults is increasing at a frightening rate. The same applies for obesity, which is becoming a major focus of concern for policy makers, given the serious health complications it generates. Don't just take it from me; do your own research into the short-term and long-term effects of caffeine and sugar, and, particularly during times of stress, limit your intake of both!

Obtain helpful support if appropriate to do so Social support has long been identified as one of the most useful resources for coping with stress. I think it depends, however, on the ability of the person you choose to confide in to hear your story without judgement and without falling into unhelpful behaviour such as reassuring or over-protecting. That is why I would emphasise the word 'helpful'. Good role models for coping with anxiety are not necessarily the people who never, ever seem to get upset or anxious. The literature on stress emphasises the benefits of good social support structures at work, and yet often school staff-rooms are not at all supportive. Why is this? Perhaps it may be to do with the solitary nature of the job of teaching. Teachers often do not have a sense of how others are doing and looking for support can be seen as a sign of weakness. I have visited many staff-rooms over the past twenty years and over-heard many pupil focused conversations but not one in which a teacher honestly spoke about the trauma she had just endured with a particular class and how she needed to change her approach in some way.

Many other professionals do not behave in this way. While firemen, police and medical personnel are expected as part of their work to put their own feelings aside and deal with day-to-day events as well as horrific emergencies, they are not expected to bury them or totally deny their existence! Policemen often work in twos, nurses have a 'hand-over meeting' and there is a general acceptance that the tougher the job, the more impact it can have on the individual staff member.

There does not seem to be the same recognition of this in the school settings. On any one day at least one teacher can have an incident where she feels attacked – by the students, parents or other teachers. To look for support for this is to wave a flag saying 'I can't cope'. Contrast that with the job of a clinical psychologist, where supervision is seen as essential and good practice. 'Supervision' – from a teacher's perspective the word may imply keeping a close eye on someone who does not really know how to do her job properly. Surely one of the hallmarks of a good teacher is that she can do her job without the need for supervision?

As part of my clinical psychology training programme I spent four months in Oxford, which is recognised as the European Centre for Cognitive-Behavioural Therapy. I was fortunate to have as my supervisor a very skilled, caring clinical psychologist, Dr Gillian Butler. Our weekly individual sessions focused on helping me learn how to use the skills of cognitive-behavioural therapy to best help my individual clients. They also helped me look at the role I played in the therapy sessions and helped me to be aware that at times my reactions to a client were more to do with me, than with him. Therefore I needed a safe, supportive environment to look at my own 'issues' in relation to the job – my feelings of being drained, dismissed or placed on a pedestal by various clients. In between these set sessions, Dr Butler was always available to support, advise and listen. As a trainee clinician these supervision sessions were essential, for my clients as well as for me. Just as we do not let a Learner Driver take a car out on her own on a motorway it is fundamental that people in therapy training programmes of all kinds receive good, regular supervision.

While in Oxford I was also fortunate and privileged to take part in the weekly 'Peer Supervision' sessions. This involved all members of the Clinical Psychology Department and was a huge learning experience for me. Everyone, from the Head of the Department down to the newly qualified clinician, took turns to present cases they were experiencing difficulties with. They presented their difficulties honestly and did not try to hide or minimise anything they had done to make the situation difficult. They were often as hard on themselves and as self-critical as I, the complete novice, was. They minimised the great work they had done and focused on the one client whom they felt had made them feel inferior, or useless or, perhaps worse, superior. It was a complete revelation to sit among those very well respected, eminent psychologists, world-experts in their field, and hear them describe their frustration, hopes and difficulties in such an honest way. The other members of the Department listened. They really listened – serious about understanding the precise difficulty and the precise meaning of that difficulty to their colleague. They did not jump in with advice, or dismiss their concerns with comments such as 'If you think that was bad, wait until you hear what happened to me ...' No, they listened and helped their colleague work through the particular difficulty in a respectful, caring way.

Now, as a more experienced clinician I consider regular supervision (i.e. at least an hour every fortnight) to be invaluable. I still believe that the word 'supervision' is not accurate – instead it is professional support at the highest level. I am very fortunate to have a highly skilled supervisor who is also exceptionally kind. She has further psychotherapy training, in addition to her training and experience as a Senior Clinical Psychologist, and brings a totally different perspective to help me better deal with challenges I encounter through my work. She also knows me very well and uses her own clinical skills and 'unconditional positive regard' to create an environment where I feel supported and safe to discuss my own feelings in relation to my work. I leave my sessions with her affirmed, re-energised and without doubt much better able to work with my own clients.

So, yes, obtaining helpful support is essential. By 'helpful' I mean someone who will listen, without judgement, without the desire to 'please' and most definitely without the desire to 'fix'. Perhaps it is unrealistic to expect individual schools to provide such support – maybe it is the role of teachers' centres or teachers' associations. The supervisors would possibly need training and ongoing support for themselves. Some schools have a mentoring system and while this can be very beneficial, it might facilitate a 'hierarchical support structure' that is totally at odds with my experience in Oxford. Some universities have recently begun to provide post-graduate courses such as Higher Diplomas and Masters in Supervision and it is heartening to see that guidance counsellors working in schools are actively pursuing supervision on a regular basis.

You probably know what I mean by the term 'unhelpful support'. We all know someone who has confided in someone else, only to have her trust shattered when her story is repeated to someone else. Support is unhelpful if it reinforces in some way an individual's own sense of inadequacy. One of the best books I have ever read is *When Helping You is Hurting Me. Escaping the Messiah Trap* by Renee Berry (1988). The author describes how seductive it can be to 'help' someone else. It can feed a need to be liked, to be valued, to be needed – and can become an addiction. Think of someone who runs out of petrol on a dark, wet evening. She phones a friend who immediately drives out to rescue her. He brings her to a garage, fills fuel into a can, drives her back and possibly brings her for a drink afterwards. A true friend. But what if she continues to drive her car without checking the petrol gauge and so many times experiences her car chugging to a halt? Sooner or later she needs to learn to take responsibility – the longer her friend is prepared to come and rescue her, the longer it is going to take her to learn to check her fuel gauge, *before* she goes on long journeys! What about her friendship? Yes, it is great to be needed. In the beginning her rescuer probably feels very good about himself – he has helped a friend in need – A true friend! But, how might he feel when he gets the thirtieth call from her – exasperated, angry, annoyed? He may well arrive out to 'help' her, but is he?

Gender differences have been noted in relation to support. Women, we are told, like to discuss their problems over and over and over. They might know the solution, or might know there is no solution, but they find comfort in discussing the problem anyway. Men, we are told, do not like this approach. They see a problem as needing a solution. They will listen, carefully and compassionately the *first* time, and will generously spend time going over various possibilities, until they come up with 'the solution'. Men, we are told (and some women may in fact have experienced this!), then get quite annoyed if the women do not solve the problem, but continue to want to discuss it and discuss it and discuss it.

So, even though the literature emphasises the role of social support in helping people cope with stress, I would caution against anyone seeking this out indiscriminately. Ideally the whole culture of the educational system would change to become supportive – in the meantime, it behoves each of us to seek out others who are genuinely, truly supportive and who choose to be. This works both ways – how genuine is your support for your colleagues?

Break large tasks down into achievable tasks This is a more obvious 'helpful action' and one which most teachers have little difficulty with. A large part of our job is breaking material our students may find complex into smaller, more manageable pieces. We do it for them, but how often do we find it impossible to do it for ourselves? Often if we allow ourselves to focus on our anxious thoughts we can become terrified by the immensity of what we need to achieve. Obvious and simple as this action might seem, it is often easier said than done. Certainly people can break complex tasks down into smaller pieces, and can often achieve these quite easily. In my experience a difficulty arises when we are unable to acknowledge our achievements, small as they may be, as a success. It really does defeat the purpose of the exercise if we achieve a small task only to berate ourselves that we did not do it long ago, or dismiss it as 'only' minimising it and making it insignificant. It is vitally important that we genuinely acknowledge every little step of achievement along the road as a success! When we can genuinely acknowledge and appreciate our own achievements, small though they may be compared to our main goals, then we can better help our students appreciate theirs.

Encourage and reward for effort as well as for success   This step is possibly the most difficult in our achievement-focused world. Our students are surrounded by 'instant gratification' and many of them do not realise how normal it is to struggle before success is achieved. You probably have come across several children in your classes who dismiss their efforts as 'useless' if they do not reach their own standards. Children and adults who experience excessive anxiety generally are very hard on themselves and do need to be taught to recognise, appreciate and reward their efforts separately from their success. This can also be easier said than done.

The condition of anxiety is seen as separate from that of depression. However, someone who has anxiety may well be at risk of developing depression, and vice versa. Therefore it makes sense that in working to relieve stress we are as familiar with the key aspects of both to put into practice as many 'Helpful Actions' as possible. Therefore, we will now turn to examine the condition of depression a little closer.

Key aspects of the nature of depression

1   There is so much pressure on students to be 'happy'.
2   Depression can be linked with experiences of anxiety, grief, eating disorders, substance abuse and illness.
3   The constant smiles of the 'class clown' may mask depression.
4   More girls report feelings of depression, but more young men commit suicide.
5   The moods of some people lift considerably when they have finally decided to commit suicide.
6   Not everyone who attempts or commits suicide has depression.
7   Students who have experienced the death of someone through suicide can be at risk themselves.
8   If a student in your school commits suicide there is a real danger of 'copy-cat' suicide.
9   Students who bullied or fought with a student who committed suicide can be at risk.

Let's look at these points in a little more detail:

There is so much pressure on students to be 'happy'

Schooldays are the happiest time of our life – or so we are told. Yet remember back to your own schooldays. Do you remember the feelings of isolation, confusion, worry? Do you remember the stabs of anxiety when you realised that you might not be as popular as you thought you were, or as clever, or as liked? What did you do? My bet is that most of you did exactly what I did – put a smile on and pretended to ourselves as well as the world that we were 'happy'. Why? The smile protected us from other people's concern and worry. It made other people feel relaxed and happy in turn and it meant that we could hide any 'negative' feelings away without having to experience them. Yet, it does not make sense for any student attending school to be happy all of the time. Just think of the pressures – the pressure to fit in, to be accepted, to make friends; the pressure to learn and to learn well and fast; the pressure not to be 'too good' or 'too liked' by the teachers so as not to become ostracised by the other students. This pressure may be familiar to all secondary school students, but even parents of five-year-old children have told me about how determined their children are to be 'good' and not 'bold'. It is desperately sad that children this young are experiencing such pressure.

What are we doing as adults and as teachers if we teach our children that they must be 'happy' all of the time, and that there is something wrong if they are unhappy? How can we be surprised then if they grow up believing that there is something terribly wrong with being unhappy? Surely it is no surprise that many children in our classes cope with pain, loneliness and unhappiness by smiling and pretending that nothing is wrong. They smile and pretend, but secretly believe that there is something inherently wrong with them because they are unhappy.

Depression can be linked with experiences of anxiety, grief, eating disorders, substance abuse and illness

Depression has been found to co-exist with a number of conditions such as anxiety, grief, eating disorders, substance abuse and illness. At times it is difficult to ascertain which comes first – does a person develop a drinking problem because they developed a dependency on drink to 'drown their sorrows', or do they have depression as a result of their dependency on drink? At other times it is easier to see how the meaning for a condition such as terminal cancer, for example, may lead a person into thinking unhelpful thoughts, engaging in unhelpful action such as avoiding friends and ultimately lead to feelings of depression. It is important therefore for us to constantly challenge our own preconceptions of what depression is.

The constant smiles of the 'class clown' may mask depression

This is true. Students who smile constantly may either deliberately mask their feelings of unhappiness, or they may be so unaware of how they actually feel that they think they are happy and are terrified and confused by any internal indications to the contrary. Feelings are messages to the body and in my mind if a feeling makes sense it is OK. It does not make sense for me to have a student in a class, in a school, who never, ever seems unhappy or in bad form. The student who takes on the role of the 'class clown' does so at the very high cost of hiding his feelings of sadness, anxiety, loneliness, anger and unhappiness. He does get a pay-back – the laughter and encouragement of the other children. He might even become dependent on those feelings for his own feelings of worth and well-being. This then makes it even more difficult for him to let the smile slip and seem unhappy. Teachers can also depend on the class clown to lighten their day and can unknowingly make it even more difficult for this student to admit to being unhappy.

A young man in his early twenties was interviewed on a national TV programme about the internationally well-publicised breakdown of his marriage. Several times during the interview he explained that he was not happy – he spoke about 'having to' be happy and that if he was not happy, there was something seriously wrong. If he could not make himself happy then how could he make his wife and children happy? For him, the solution was to end his marriage. Many students share that sense that there is something seriously wrong with them if they are unhappy. They learn to hide their feelings of unhappiness by smiling, but find that the internal pressure just gets to be too much. For too many of them the only solution they see is to take their own lives.

More girls report feelings of depression, but more young men commit suicide

This is a well-reported fact in the international literature on depression. In self-report measures significantly more women than men, girls than boys, report feelings and/or symptoms of depression. The statistics still show that more men commit suicide than women, although the gap is decreasing. Is this a paradox? I think we must look at how depression is measured. The *Beck Depression Inventory* (Beck, 1978) is a reliable and valid self-report instrument for measuring depression. The *Children's Depression Inventory* (Kovacs, 1992) is used to measure depression in children. Both of these are self-report measures and rely on the person completing them to tell the truth about how they are feeling. As we have seen, some people actually do not know how they are feeling and prefer to believe that they are 'fine' and have 'no problems'. In general girls talk about their problems, and their feelings about their problems, more than boys do. Boys and men are, as a rule, more action oriented. If there is a problem – problem solve – decide what to do and do it. Many 'pop psychology' books such as *Men are from Mars, Women are from Venus* (Gray, 1992) have been written to guide men and women in understanding how this basic difference can have such an impact on relationships.

Yet we don't actually know if women and girls experience depression more than men and boys. A few years ago over 700 twelve and thirteen-year-old students participated in a research study I was carrying out in seven schools with the support and help of the guidance counsellors, principals, parents and students (Hayes and Morgan, 2005; Hayes, 2001a, 2001b).

Its aim was to prevent depression in adolescents using a school-based psychoeducational programme. The first step was to establish the level of depression in that age-group and so the students, with their parents' permission, agreed to complete the *Children's Depression Inventory* (Kovacs, 1992), the *Porteous Problem Checklist* (Porteous, 1997) and a questionnaire I designed specifically for the purpose of the research: 50 per cent of the students were female and 50 per cent were male. As expected, and consistent with the literature, significantly more girls than boys reported feelings of depression, reported that they worried and said that they needed help in coping. However, there was one very interesting, unexpected finding to the question: 'How do you worry compared to your peers? Do you worry a lot more, a bit more, the same, a bit less or a lot less?' We might have expected more boys than girls to say that they worried a lot less than their peers. Interestingly this was not the case. Significantly more boys than girls said that they worried a lot more than their peers. No, they did not report feelings of depression, no, they did not worry, but actually, they worried a lot more than their peers.

What is the explanation for this apparent contradiction? I think it lies in the fact that girls do talk about their feelings to their peers. Therefore while they may see themselves as having problems, they know that their friends have problems too and so they do not get as worried about it as they might otherwise do. Boys, on the other hand, may not realise that other boys have worries and problems too. As no one talks about them, a young boy may feel that he is the only one who is not coping. Over time the pressure to keep up an appearance of coping may be too great. Is it any wonder, therefore, that suicide seems to be the only option?

The moods of some people lift considerably when they have finally decided to commit suicide

This is a warning sign for suicide that can be easy to miss. When we think about it, it actually is not that surprising. A few years ago I had a very difficult decision to make – would I stay in a particular job or would I leave. There were many reasons why I should stay and I did not have a particular job in mind that I wanted to go to. For months I debated the 'pros' and 'cons' of staying and of leaving. I would go into work on a Monday morning determined that yes, I was right to leave. Then three lovely things would happen which would remind me of how much I enjoyed my work and would make me reconsider. Then I would decide that because I did not know where I wanted to go to I would stay until I did. That decision would be comforting only until something occurred to remind me that really, despite my best efforts to fit in and be happy, I was a round peg in a square hole – the best, but scariest, solution was to give notice and leave. This process continued on a daily basis for about six months. It was exhausting. It was also very isolating as I did not feel I could discuss this decision with my colleagues. The danger I saw in confiding and seeking social support was that if I decided to stay, my colleagues might perceive me as someone who was not totally committed, who did not really want to be there and who was only waiting for a better opportunity to come along. So for months I felt a fraud when I participated in planning meetings not knowing if I was actually going to be there to follow through on various plans. I will never forget the relief of actually reaching the final decision and giving notice. The heaviness of the months of anguish and indecision lifted. I felt so much lighter and at peace and was aware that some might misinterpret this as delight in leaving. That was not the case as the actual leaving a job I really liked to face uncertainty was not easy, so I am clear that the huge relief I left was due to my internal torture as a result of my indecision being ended.

If I could experience that enormous sense of relief over a job, how must it be for someone who has had the huge decision of whether to take his own life? I cannot imagine the months of internal torture – the moments spent weighing up the difficulties of living with the attraction of death; the feelings of pain, fear, anger, despair, hopelessness. But I can in some tiny way appreciate how a person can suddenly feel so much lighter and freer when he has finally resolved his internal battle and has made his decision. So, yes, as teachers, we must learn to wonder why a particular student is suddenly in such good form, and to act on our puzzlement.

Not everyone who attempts or commits suicide has depression

This is another very important point. Professionals working in the area of suicide distinguish between suicide and parasuicide. If someone attempts to take his own life and does not succeed it is invaluable to determine as far as possible if he was actually suicidal or if his suicide attempt was parasuicidal. What is the difference? If a person is genuinely suicidal, he will more likely than not seek to end his life again. If he is parasuicidal, he may be so relieved to be still alive that he will never make another attempt. Remember my emphasis on the meaning of the event. Someone who is suicidal may interpret his 'failed suicide attempt' as further proof that he is a complete useless failure. This, combined with the upset, concern and fear of those around him, can serve to make him feel even more distressed and he can begin once again to plan how to end his life. But what about the person who was not actually genuinely suicidal? The person who attempted suicide on a whim, an impulse, a 'cry for help'? Remember my emphasis on beliefs. It is very important that he is helped to come to terms with his suicide attempt in a way that does not create a belief that he is in fact 'suicidal'. The consequences of this particular self-fulfilling prophecy can be tragic. Therefore, while it is understandable that family members, friends and teachers will be wary and watchful, the saying that 'if someone attempts suicide once he will do it again' is not necessarily true. If someone who is not suicidal believes it however, it is not difficult to see how he can convince himself that he is and make another attempt to take his own life.

How can we tell if someone is suicidal or parasuicidal? Psychiatrists have a very important role in assessing a person's state of mind after a suicide attempt. Naturally the meaning of being seen by a psychiatrist varies for people and for some is further proof that there is something seriously wrong with them and that they are 'mad'. In reality a psychiatric assessment following a suicide attempt is essential in assessing the survivor's risk of making a second attempt. This can be extraordinarily difficult and therefore is not for the teacher or the family member to do. Some differences have been noticed – a person who is genuinely suicidal is more likely to plan the event carefully, to use extreme methods and to show a lightness of mood shortly before making the attempt. The person who is parasuicidal is more likely to act on impulse, without definite plans, and may show no obvious difference in mood.

Students who have experienced the death of someone through suicide can be at risk themselves. If a student in your school commits suicide there is a real danger of 'copy-cat' suicide

This is a very important point for teachers to be aware of. Tragically there are many examples of schools where 'copy-cat' suicides occur following the suicide of a student. Why is this? There are no definite answers. I used to say to student teachers that I would love to go to the moon as a tourist. At the time that was an idea that just could not be carried out. I would then ask them to imagine that a close family member or friend told me that he had tickets to go to the moon and went. Suddenly my limits of what is possible and impossible would totally change. Suddenly going to the moon would come into my immediate world and would become an option for me too. Since I started using that example people have in fact gone to the moon as tourists – it is still too expensive for me to consider, but the idea has moved from being totally impossible, to a 'maybe'.

There is an ongoing debate as to the wisdom of talking openly about suicide to young people. Could it put the idea into their heads? Could it become an acceptable, logical option for them? Was it better when suicide was a taboo subject, which was associated with shame? Experts in the area of suicide are clear that talking about suicide does not put the idea into students' heads. I do wonder though about the effect on vulnerable students who attend the funeral of one of their friends who has died by suicide. If we normalise the option of suicide, are we at risk for making the choice too available to others? I believe it is important, vitally important, to discuss with the class-mates of a student who has committed suicide the meaning and the impact of them on what has happened. How are they feeling? What are they thinking and what are they doing? This point is developed further in the Action section below.

Students who bullied or fought with a student who committed suicide can be at risk

It is obvious that the siblings and friends of someone who has committed suicide will be affected and may be at risk for 'copying' the act. It is less obvious, but possibly more likely, that the students who did not like the victim, who may have bullied him, can also be at risk. It is not as easy for them to show their upset, their horror and their confusion. They may blame themselves for the death, they may feel others blame them and the internal and external blame may be too much – so teachers, in the tragic event that one of your students commits suicide, be alert to the needs of all of the students who are left to cope – the enemies, as well as the friends.

Helpful actions to cope with depression

The 'Coping Triangle' is a simple tool for helping us to identify our thoughts, feelings and actions in relation to a particular stressor. We then ask ourselves if our feelings make sense, and examine our thoughts and actions to see if they are helpful or unhelpful. At that point it is essential that we *do* something helpful! Blaming ourselves for having so many unhelpful thoughts and actions is unhelpful. Deciding that we are 'hopeless cases' is also unhelpful! Blaming ourselves and/or others for our current situation? Unhelpful! Dwelling on the awfulness of it all? Unhelpful. Turning to addictive behaviours such as overeating and/or drinking excessively? Unhelpful. Putting our heads in the sand and pretending that things are fine? Unhelpful.

I could go on. There is an infinite list of unhelpful actions we can take in response to thoughts, feelings and actions, which can lead us further along the road to the condition of depression. Anybody can get depression. Anybody. All we need to do is to begin to decrease our level of helpful actions, to focus on how awful we are feeling, to worry that there is something seriously wrong with us, to lose interest in pursuing social activities, to become frightened by our hopeless, frightened, harsh thoughts, and to become trapped in a downward spiral, as is illustrated by the depression 'Coping Triangle' in Figure 7.1.

If unhelpful actions increase our feelings of depression and encourage us to think even more unhelpful thoughts, it makes sense that 'Helpful Actions' will do the reverse and interrupt the downward spiral of depression. Knowing what to do is not enough – we must really act in as helpful a way as possible. As you read the various suggestions below be aware of your

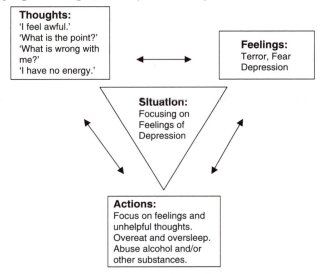

Figure 7.1 The depression 'Coping Triangle'

own thoughts and feelings, as they are great indicators of how willing you are to act in a helpful way!

Helpful actions in coping with depression include

1 Accept that being 'unhappy' is normal.
2 Recognise that depression can be linked with experiences of anxiety, grief, eating disorders, substance abuse and illness.
3 Be aware that 'unhappiness' and depression can be masked by a smile.
4 Determine the meaning of the depression for you.
5 Refer student to school guidance counsellor or outside agency if appropriate.
6 Help students cope with feelings of unhappiness in appropriate ways.
7 Teach students the role that feelings, thoughts and actions have in depression.
8 Help students realise that they do not have to act on their thoughts.
9 Obtain helpful support from colleagues and/or appropriate professionals.
10 Be aware of the risk of suicide.

These points are developed further below.

Accept that being 'unhappy' is normal

This may be easier said than done. From a very young age we have all grown up with fairy tales that ended with 'and they all lived happily ever after'.

Also from a very young age most children learn that adults are more pleased with us when we are happy than when we are sad. Interestingly, however, some children learn that it is nice to be sad, because then they get cuddled or bought things to 'cheer up'. We can understand this if we consider the meaning to the adult in question. I have worked with some parents who have had harsh memories of their own childhoods and they are determined that their child will have a 'happy childhood'. So, some children learn that it is not OK to be sad or unhappy. Others learn that being sad is nice because of what happens afterwards, but that it is still not 'normal'. And yet, what are we teaching our children if we do not allow them the opportunity to feel sadness and to cope with it?

Many people are familiar with the story of Bridget Jones by Helen Fielding. At the end of the first book and film *Bridget Jones's Diary: A Novel* (Fielding, 2001) we see the heroine being swept off her feet by a very handsome Mr Darcy. 'Ahh,' we might think – 'and they live happily ever after!' But wait, the beginning of the second book and film *Bridget Jones: The Return to Reason* (Fielding, 2004) starts with the heroine six weeks into her new relationship with her hero. How is she feeling? What is she thinking? What is she doing? Let's look at Figure 7.2 'Bridget's Coping Triangle':

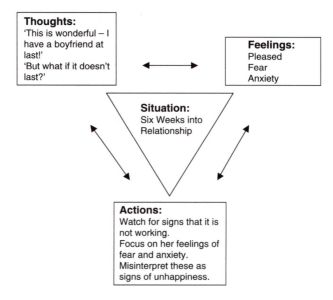

Figure 7.2 Bridget's Coping Triangle

So what has happened? Bridget's initial feelings of pleasure have been replaced by fear and anxiety that the relationship is not going to last for long. Her thoughts are more than likely linked to an underlying belief that she does not deserve to have a relationship with someone like Mark Darcy in the first place and that it will never work out. She begins to feel anxious, fearful and unhappy. She seizes on these feelings as proof that the relationship is not working and as the story unfolds, the self-fulfilling prophecy becomes clear. Somehow Bridget does not seem to realise that it is OK to be fearful and at times unhappy. She, like many of us, has the belief that she has to be happy and that her happiness is completely dependent on her being loved by a man like Mark Darcy. What pressure! No wonder she is seen resorting to food as a comfort and beginning to display signs of depression. But does she learn? The end of the second film finds her back in the arms of Mark Darcy accepting his proposal of marriage – and we can assume that she expects to live 'happily ever after'.

We might hope that the students in our class realise that life is not like that. I do not think we can assume it. Feeling unhappy is not a nice feeling. It makes sense that we might try to ignore, avoid or deny it. But think of it like a tooth-ache. The pain is telling us that there is something wrong. If we blame the tooth-ache without taking steps to look at what is causing the pain, the pain gets worse. Being unhappy is part and parcel of the richness and diversity of life. Using the 'Coping Sentence' helps us to acknowledge the feeling, without getting frightened or shamed by it, and allows us to focus on something helpful that is also true.

So, a possible 'Coping Sentence' for Bridget Jones: 'I feel unhappy because I think that this relationship might not last, *but I might be wrong!*'

Instead of focusing predominantly on feelings and judging them as wrong or negative or shameful, let us instead acknowledge them as making sense in the particular situation and then turn instead to pay attention to helpful thoughts and helpful actions such as those described below.

Recognise that depression can be linked with experiences of anxiety, grief, eating disorders, substance abuse and illness

This recognition is important in enabling us to be more tolerant of the complexity of our feelings as well as those of our students and our colleagues. It can also help us be vigilant when we are experiencing anxiety and/or other difficulties to work to prevent depression developing. Sometimes feelings of depression are healthy, normal reactions to upsetting, traumatic or awful encounters. Who among us would not worry about a young woman who professes being 'thrilled' that she was brutally gang raped? Surely it is more normal as well as healthier for her to have strong feelings of anger, depression and anxiety. Often, however, these 'normal' feelings are hidden and denied. They can then fester and trigger the beginnings of the condition of Depression.

*Be aware that 'unhappiness' and depression can be masked
by a smile*

This is self-explanatory. As teachers we do need to be on the alert that
students who constantly smile, who are always in good form and who are
always 'fine' may actually be masking severe depression. How can we tell?
We can ask ourselves if it is appropriate that the student is smiling – e.g.
when they have not done as well in an exam as they had expected, or when
one of their friends stops talking to them, or when a parent is ill.

Determine the meaning of the depression for you

This step involves taking some time to consider carefully the meaning of
depression for you so that you are not over- or under-reacting to the mood
of the students in your care. You can do this by becoming informed about
depression through reading books such as those listed in Chapter 8 and/
or doing some personal self-development work with an appropriate
professional.

*Refer student to school guidance counsellor or outside agency
if appropriate*

It can be difficult to know when to refer a child for professional treatment.
The clearer a teacher is about her reaction to depression the better she is at
separating out her needs and concerns from those of the child. Some schools
will have a school guidance counsellor who will advise as to whether a
referral to an outside agency is appropriate. Other schools will not and
therefore this decision must be taken carefully in consultation with the
School Principal and the child's parents.

*Help students cope with feelings of unhappiness in
appropriate ways*

The first step in coping with the feelings of unhappiness appropriately is to
acknowledge them. The second is to express them if it is safe to do so, either
through crying or in writing or drawing. This is tricky, as there is a fine
balance between expressing feelings of unhappiness and wallowing in them.
How can we tell? Use the 'frequency, duration and intensity' guide. Let us
suppose that a student in the class committed suicide. It makes absolute
sense that the other students would be shocked, upset and traumatised.
It makes absolute sense that the deceased student's girl-friend would get
upset and would frequently break down and cry. In the beginning her upset
would be very frequent, very intense and last for some time. We would
expect that over time, the episodes would become less frequent, less intense
and shorter. If not, then we need to act. Obviously in an extreme example

like this one the girl in question would receive additional support from the school's guidance counsellor and/or outside professionals.

Let's take a less dramatic example. A student has just obtained a grade lower than he had expected. He smiles, says he is fine, and says it does not matter. Ideally students could become familiar with the 'Coping Triangle' themselves so that such a student can have a way of accessing his thoughts as well as his feelings. Then, instead of pretending to himself that he is fine, he would be able to realise that his anxious, unhappy feelings make sense given that he is thinking 'I will never get into college now'; 'My father is going to be so disappointed with me'; or 'I have let myself down'. He can then use the 'Coping Sentence' to help him make sense of his feelings such as 'I feel upset because of my low grade *but I choose not to give myself a hard time over it*'.

The question of the teacher's role comes into play. Is it really part of the teacher's role to help a student cope with depression? I believe it is in the wider sense, but it is important that teachers respect boundaries and their own levels of competence. Classroom teachers are not trained counsellors.

Teach students the role that feelings, thoughts and actions have in depression

The core cognitive-behavioural principles are so simple but effective we might wonder why we did not learn them when we were five years old. There are many books on cognitive-behavioural therapy for professionals and lay people and some of these are listed in the next chapter. However, as teachers are not therapists it is important that students are not subjected to teachers 'practising' cognitive-behavioural techniques on them to 'treat' a particular condition. A little knowledge can indeed be a dangerous thing, and we must be constantly aware of the boundaries of our role. Within those boundaries though we do have a lot of scope to use cognitive-behavioural principles in an educational, preventative way.

One of my loveliest experiences as a teacher was a month I spent working in a School for Children with Special Needs. Each morning the School Principal, a wonderful, vibrant, kind lady, played her guitar while the children took turns at singing their favourite songs. One little boy sang the same song every day – 'Do what you do do well, boys – do, what you do do well'. Those words have had a strong impact on me – much more so than any bits of wisdom I have gleaned from family, friends, teachers or books. As teachers we teach – so let us 'do it well'. It is not within our remit to use cognitive-behavioural principles to 'treat' students, but we can teach the core principles, so that they have a very practical but effective tool to help themselves cope with stressors and challenges as they emerge.

One way of doing this is to take an example the students will identify with. For a young child it might be asking a group of children if he can play and being told 'no'. An example older students might identify with is entering the school corridor and noticing a group of students who stop laughing when they see him. You could draw the 'Coping Triangle' and ask the students to suggest how they might feel, think and act in that situation. This could be discussed in a large class group or alternatively students can work together in small groups. Key cognitive-behavioural principles to emphasise are listed in Table 7.1.

Table 7.1 Key cognitive-behavioural principles

General	The meaning of something is important and can be different for everyone. The meaning is based on someone's own experience, attitudes, and beliefs.
Feelings	Are messages telling us what is going on in our bodies? They are neither 'good' nor 'bad', 'positive' nor 'negative'. If a feeling makes sense it is OK. We can cope with our feelings in helpful or unhelpful ways. Unhelpful ways include blaming ourselves for having the feelings, pretending that they do not exist, or obsessing and examining our feelings over and over. Helpful ways include recognising them, acknowledging them to ourselves, accepting them gently and expressing them safely.
Thoughts	We think thoughts a lot. We think the same thoughts a lot. We often believe our thoughts without question. Thoughts can be 'helpful' or 'unhelpful'. 'Unhelpful thoughts' often include words like 'should', e.g. 'I should not have said that.' Unhelpful thoughts can be like a harsh, critical, judgemental voice in our head. Unhelpful thoughts are unhelpful if they keep us locked in a cycle where we think unhelpful thoughts, do unhelpful actions, feel bad, think more unhelpful thoughts, feel worse, do less, etc. We often believe our unhelpful thoughts without question. Just because we think something does not make it true. Not thinking is impossible. Blaming ourselves for having unhelpful thoughts is not helpful. We can learn to pay less attention to unhelpful thoughts. We can learn to focus on helpful thoughts.
Actions	Actions can also be helpful or unhelpful. Helpful actions break the cycle of unhelpful critical thoughts that can lead us to feeling attacked and criticised. Unhelpful actions such as over-eating can lead to unhelpful thoughts such as 'I am such a pig' which can lead to us feeling horrible, which can lead to more unhelpful thoughts such as 'Well, I might as well just keep going and finish the whole lot now', which then leads to more unhelpful action! A helpful action can be to give 'life' to the harsh critical voice by naming it, describing it, drawing it and also to give 'life' to a compassionate, encouraging voice in the same way. Other helpful actions can include writing thoughts out on paper, to 'get them out of our heads' so as to examine them and see if we actually believe them.
Beliefs	Beliefs are incredibly powerful. What we believe becomes our reality. Often we learn to believe something as a means to protecting ourselves, but continue to believe it long after it is true or helpful. Some beliefs which can cause great distress are: – The world is a dangerous place – I am unlovable, useless, worthless – I am weak and need to be minded – It is my fault – I don't deserve love What we believe is true – for us. People believed for centuries that the world was flat. The world is round – not flat!

Help students realise that they do not have to act on their thoughts

This step involves teaching students to 'problem solve', to be creative and to take responsibility for their actions. It is so important to teach students that just because they think life is not worth living, that does not inevitably mean that they have no choice but to commit suicide. Just because they think they would like a drink does not mean that they have no choice but to drink, etc. Many students have not had practice in actually making decisions and taking responsibility for these. We need to allow them to learn this at a very young age.

Obtain helpful support from colleagues and/or appropriate professionals

The point has been made, but I will make it again. Teaching is a very demanding job, with little recognition of the need for helpful support from colleagues and/or appropriate professionals. Teachers with depression have told me with amazement how they could not believe that colleagues saw them as always being in great form, always calm, relaxed, always confident, always capable. One of their big concerns was around how they could continue to hide the fact that they had depression, and how the teachers would react if they knew. Teachers are people too. They have busy, demanding jobs and busy, demanding lives. Many of them are extremely harsh, critical and judgemental of themselves and crucify themselves on a daily basis with all kinds of savage thoughts. Is it any surprise that many teachers suffer from depression? Is it any surprise that some of their students may suffer as a result of their depression? But where is the acceptance, the tolerance, the support?

Be aware of the risk of suicide

This point is listed last, but that is not intended to denote lack of emphasis or importance. As described above, students who cannot separate their thoughts from their actions can be at risk from suicide. So can their teachers. This risk can increase if they have additional pressures, with weak internal and/or external supports. It can also increase if they have experienced the death of someone who has committed suicide in their family, or class-mates. It is easier to be aware of the risk of suicide in someone who is constantly down, looks miserable and talks incessantly about how easier everyone's lives would be if he was not here, and how he wishes he had the courage to 'just do it'. It is much more difficult to realise that the student, or teacher, who is constantly in great form, irrespective of life events, may be at risk. Therefore, teachers, be aware, and if you are concerned ACT! Act by discussing your concerns with the School Principal. If you are the School Principal it is wise to have a School

Policy on this very matter. My advice is that you notify the child's parents about your concerns and recommend that he be seen by his medical doctor. If your concern is about a teacher, my advice is to speak directly to the teacher and discuss your concerns with him. You could show him the 'Coping Triangle' or even lend him this book. But be aware – and act!

Tables 7.2 and 7.3 contain a summary of the key points to help yourself and others cope with anxiety and depression.

Table 7.2 Key points about anxiety and depression

Anxiety	
	• The experience of anxiety is normal.
	• It is a learned response to external or internal events that we perceive as threatening.
	• Many of us label feelings of anxiety as 'weak'.
	• Some of us focus anxiously on the feelings of anxiety – the result is understandably greater anxiety!
	• People who feel anxious often are extremely self-critical and berate themselves as 'stupid'.
	• Anxiety left unaided can and does increase in frequency, duration and intensity.
	• Reassuring someone who is experiencing anxiety that 'they will be fine' does not work!
	• Reassurance actually only makes the anxiety more intense.
	• Anxiety left unaided can and does increase in frequency, duration and intensity.
Depression	
	• It makes sense that we will feel unhappy sometimes.
	• We can accept our feelings of unhappiness, fight them, run away from them or blame ourselves for having them.
	• Choosing to blame ourselves for feeling down and feeling unhappy is unhelpful.
	• Being gentle and compassionate with ourselves is helpful.
	• Focusing incessantly on how we feel is unhelpful.
	• It makes sense that we will feel unhappy sometimes.
	• Acknowledging how we feel and then doing something helpful, such as going for a walk in the fresh air, is more helpful.
	• If we go for a walk and allow ourselves to listen to unhelpful thoughts such as 'I am so unfit', 'I knew this would not work', 'everyone is looking at me' we will probably not get the benefits of the exercise!

What have you learned from that exercise? Table 7.4 contains a sample of some possible responses.

Table 7.3 Coping with anxiety and depression involves the following

Anxiety	1	Acknowledge the feelings of anxiety.
	2	Link them to something which makes sense.
	3	Identify scary, unhelpful thoughts which only make the anxiety worse.
	4	Deliberately think more helpful thoughts such as the 'Coping Sentence': 'I *feel* anxious *because* the class are not taking their work seriously and their exams start next week *but I cannot do their exam for them.*'
	5	Change unhelpful actions such as avoidance by deliberately beginning to face the fear, or engaging in distraction techniques, or seeking helpful support.
	6	Genuinely acknowledge, appreciate and reward effort over achievement.
Depression	1	Learning to gently identify thoughts as 'helpful' or 'unhelpful' can reduce the power they have on us to feel a particular way.
	2	Learn to react differently to our feelings and our thoughts.
	3	Learn to gently identify thoughts as 'helpful' or 'unhelpful' as this can reduce the power they have on us to feel a particular way.
	4	Acknowledging how we feel and then doing something helpful, such as going for a walk in the fresh air, is more helpful.

Anger

You might wonder why I have left the emotion of anger last in this chapter. Does this annoy you? Bear with me for a few moments. Think of a recent situation that triggered you to feel angry. Now complete Exercise 7.1 to become clear about your feelings, thoughts and actions around that situation.

Exercise 7.1 My 'Coping Triangle' about a situation which triggered anger

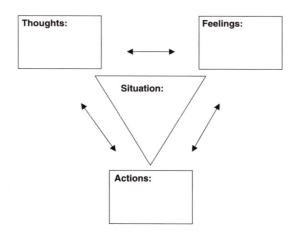

Table 7.4 Possible responses to anger

Thoughts	Feelings	Actions
I should be ashamed of myself. I am the adult.	Guilt, shame, anger at self.	Berate self severely.
Nobody understands what it is like for me and what I have to put up with every day. It is wrong and unfair.	Unsupported.	Indulge in 'self-pity'. Become defensive.
I am totally right to feel this angry. How dare he treat me that way?	Anger.	Blame other. Lash out.

The feeling of anger is not wrong. It can be a natural, healthy response to something that we find threatening, humiliating, or difficult. The feeling may well make sense, but as you might have expected me to say at this point, it is not the feeling, but how we think and act in relation to the feeling that are important. What is the meaning of the situation for us? Why do we react so quickly to some situations while managing to remain completely calm in many others? It is worth our while spending time exploring the meaning of such situations to us as well as our underlying beliefs. Teachers who tend to react in anger very quickly may have an enormous amount of stressors to cope with. In addition to numerous external ones, they also may well have internal stressors such as thoughts beginning with 'How dare he/she/they?', 'Do they think I am a fool?' or 'Everyone is out to get me'.

Thankfully as yet we do not have a specific condition called ANGER. We do, however, have medical conditions that can be a direct result of bottled up anger, such as coronary heart disease and ulcers.

Key points in learning to cope with anger are as follows

1 We can learn to respond to anger constructively.
2 Tune in to the power of language.
3 We have learned how to react to anger and we can learn to react differently.
4 The 'Coping Sentence' works in helping us use our anger effectively.
5 The calmer we are, the better able we are to cope with our anger and the anger of others.
6 Distraction can be a very effective way of not getting caught into someone's anger.

These points are developed below.

We can learn to respond to anger constructively

Imagine that you are a young child in a playground. An older child comes in and starts to threaten you verbally. What are your choices? You can run, cry, shout back or ignore. Ignoring is very difficult to do and sometimes is not an appropriate reaction. Let us suppose that you are a teacher walking by the playground and notice the older child taunting the younger child. Obviously few of us would ignore the situation. Yet, while we might feel angry, we have a duty to respond in an adult, mature way. If we pick up the older child and teach him a lesson or two physically, who has won? Nobody – the child has learned that brute force is the choice of adults and the adult has reinforced his automatic urge to lash out and hurt. So what do we do?

Tune in to the power of language

Anger is a powerful emotion. A very powerful emotion. As we have seen, if we repress it, it can cause serious difficulties such as physical ill health and can also contribute to us developing the condition of depression. We can however choose to use anger effectively. One way that might seem strange initially is to deliberately defuse the power of the anger by our use of words. Take a moment to repeat the two sentences below out loud three times.

A I am furious
B I feel a slight bit annoyed

Do you remember how I compared our feelings to men working in the bottom of a ship shovelling in coal when the captain says 'Danger'? The words we say to ourselves are very, very powerful. Yes, we may in fact be furious, but even deliberately focusing on our use of words to describe that anger can be hugely helpful in helping us to cope with it. 'But that is tricking myself and is not true,' you might say. Think for a moment about the self-fulfilling prophesy – we can tell ourselves we are furious and we can react by feeling furious so quickly, we may not realise that our reactions are due to our thoughts, rather than to the actual event!

We have learned how to react to anger and we can learn to react differently

Just think about the example of you as a young child in the playground being verbally abused by an older child. How would you have reacted? Now, how did you learn to react in that way? Was it because a parent, an older brother, or a friend taught you to react in that way? Was it because you had learned from trial and error that that was the best way to react in that situation?

We are no longer children but a lot of our supposedly 'automatic' reactions are actually learned responses. Fortunately if we learned them, we can unlearn them and learn other, more appropriate ways of responding to anger. This may take a little practice – or it might take a life-time of deliberate effort.

Occasionally when I want to illustrate how automatic our reactions can be, I scrunch up a sheet of paper and throw it at the child or adult I am working with. Generally their reactions are ones of amazement, surprise and occasionally anger. It is very interesting to see what they do next. Most of them automatically throw it back at me. I then ask them what else they could have done. They *choose* to throw the paper back at me, but could they have *chosen* to act differently? Yes, they could have thrown it away, let it fall to the ground, torn it up, etc. When I repeat the exercise and this time ask them to ignore the paper completely, many people find that despite their best efforts they automatically reach out, grab the paper and then stop themselves from throwing it back at me. It is hard, at times very hard, to break old patterns of behaviour. I then ask them to visualise the paper as a nasty comment, a sarcastic remark or a deliberately cruel insult. It is not easy to ignore such things, but we can learn to do so. Of course, our perception that the comment is nasty, the remark sarcastic or the comment an insult, may not in fact be true. Not responding automatically, defensively and aggressively allows us time to consider if our perceptions are accurate.

There may be many occasions where 'turning the other cheek' is unrealistic and unhelpful. However, deliberately choosing how we respond to our anger means that we are less likely to respond in an automatic, angry way. Buying ourselves some time means that we can consider carefully how best to respond. If possible it means that we can obtain real support for us by checking out our perceptions and obtaining advice from a trusted colleague or friend.

Responding to our feelings of anger in an angry way can be like firemen pouring petrol onto a blazing fire. It is so much better for us as well as for others if we can learn to choose to respond to our feelings of anger when we are calm.

The 'Coping Sentence' works in helping us use our anger effectively

The 'Coping Sentence' can focus us on identifying our feeling of anger, linking it to something that makes sense and then choosing to use the energy of that anger in a helpful way. Three examples of how the 'Coping Sentence' might be useful are as follows:

'I feel annoyed because I think that they are talking about me but *maybe I am wrong.*'

'I feel annoyed because two students in my class did not stop their disruptive behaviour when I told them to but *I choose to deal with them later when I am calmer.*'

'I feel annoyed because Mr Jones is blaming me for his son's bad results but *I choose not to get trapped in the blame game.*'

The calmer we are, the better able we are to cope with our anger and the anger of others

My guess is you know this already. We are all quicker to respond to other people's anger when we are tired, hungry, ill or generally not in good form. The more relaxed we are the better we can respond. Many people do not realise how tense they actually are until they begin to deliberately learn relaxation techniques such as breathing slowly, meditation and yoga. The more they practise relaxation, the quicker they can learn to recognise signs of tension in themselves, such as their jaw tightening, their hands clenching, their stomach tightening. They can then choose to deliberately focus on relaxing those parts of their body, which also can distract them from the anger of the other person. Of course, people who are in the middle of a rage can tend to become even more enraged if they sense that the person they are directing their anger towards is not getting upset. Be prepared and breathe slowly.

Distraction can be a very effective way of not getting caught into someone's anger

We all meet people who choose to respond to certain situations aggressively. We have a choice too. We can choose to also get drawn into behaving aggressively or we can choose to distance ourselves a little from the situation by distracting. We might ask ourselves questions such as: 'If I were a journalist reporting on this scene, how would I describe this?' We might deliberately choose to react with compassion towards the person. We might wonder to ourselves what the meaning of his anger is and, if appropriate, explore this meaning with him. It is helpful for us to remind ourselves that his feelings of anger more than likely make sense for him, given what he is thinking and doing, but that it might not be our position to point that out!

The past three chapters have focused on how the 'Coping Triangle' can be used to help teachers cope with their feelings of anger, anxiety and depression. Focusing on these feelings is not in any way intended to deny the existence of other emotions such as shame, guilt or embarrassment. My hope is that you are now proficient in using the 'Coping Triangle' and the 'Coping Sentence' as tools to help you relieve your stress, whatever its cause. The next chapter provides an overview of the various theories that have contributed to the development of the 'Coping Triangle' as a key tool for teachers to use to relieve their stress. I suggest that you take a little time first to try out the practical exercise below.

Exercise 7.2

Let's see how you might apply the 'Coping Triangle' to help one of your colleagues who is considering leaving teaching altogether. You were shocked to hear him react very aggressively to another teacher in a recent staff meeting. When asked to apologise by the Principal he refused and stormed out of the meeting. An hour later he returned, interrupted the meeting and told the entire staff that he has had enough and is leaving teaching. He has been a good friend of yours since you both joined the school six years ago as newly qualified teachers. Later you persuade him to meet you after school to talk about his decision.

That afternoon you listen quietly as he describes what has actually been happening in his life over the past six months. You are stunned to hear that his wife has been seriously ill and that there is still the possibility that she might have leukaemia. One of his children (aged eighteen months old) is teething and has not slept for a full night in over a month. His other child (aged four) has picked up the worry about his wife and is clearly upset. Your friend lies awake at night worrying about how he would survive if anything happens to his wife and finds himself hating her doctors for not being more positive. With very obvious shame he described even resenting his two young children for claiming so much of his wife's time.

It becomes very clear that your friend is incredibly self-critical. He gives frequent examples of how unsupportive he has been to his wife and how desperate he feels when he sees the look of hurt in his children's eyes after he has shouted at them to be quiet. Up until now he was determined that nobody outside his immediate family would know what was going on. He did not want pity or the pressure of answering well-meaning questions on a daily basis. School was really his safety net. It was the one area of his life that remained constant and he took pride from the fact that no matter how difficult things were at home, he was managing to do his work well. In fact, you quickly realise that school has become an extra pressure. Lately he has worried about what might happen if the pressure on him became too much and his work as a teacher began to be affected. He could name the parents of students in his various classes who would demand that he took time off rather than face the risk of their children's education suffering. To ensure that no one could raise any questions about his teaching ability he had begun to give extra work to his students in many classes.

As he speaks you remember the particular comment from another teacher at the staff meeting, which had sparked the aggressive reaction. 'Students' Homework' was a key item on the agenda as parents had complained about the lack of consistency in the amount of homework being given and the frequency in which homework was not corrected by the teachers. One of the Physical Education teachers had said something along the lines of 'Yes, as a parent of a student who gets far too much homework from some of you, I think we should seriously reconsider this whole thing. Some of you with young children have no idea of how much time and effort it takes night after night to ensure that homework is done. It would be nice if you gave us a break sometimes as well as our children!'

Hence the explosion!

Now, how could you use the various tools in this book to help your friend relieve his stress?

This might be an exercise you would like to do on your own and then compare your responses to those of a friend. It would be interesting to ask someone who is not a teacher and who has not read this book to do the exercise also. Prepare to meet a 'Why does he not pull himself together?' reaction! Another suggestion is to ask a trusted colleague to complete the exercise as if he/she were you. You might be surprised to learn how your colleague thinks you react in a potentially stressful situation!

In Chapter 9 we will revisit this exercise and I will list some specific areas you might want to approach. First though, try it yourself and see how you get on.

8 Theory behind the 'Coping Triangle'

Some years ago a Senior Clinical Psychologist, who was supervising me as part of my training, told me that no one could ever claim ownership of an idea, as no idea is ever completely original. At the time I was completing some research and felt very 'precious' about it being original and all of my own work. I now see that he is right. The 'Coping Triangle' is my way of presenting the basics of cognitive-behavioural theory. I cannot claim that I have discovered 'Coping'. I certainly have not been the first to use the shape of the triangle as a simple but clear way of presenting ideas visually. And I have no claim to the origins of cognitive-behavioural therapy either! This chapter was written for three reasons. One was to acknowledge the enormous work of some of the people whose theories have informed my clinical work and writing. The second was to offer a solid, theoretical basis to the 'Coping Triangle', and the third to provide some signposts if you would like to learn more. The chapter is not in any way intended to be a comprehensive, academic account of the contributions of learning theorists, cognitive-behavioural theory, coping and prevention work. It is, however, a start!

Meaning

A key tenet in this book is 'the meaning of the event, rather than the event itself, is what matters'. This idea is not new, however, and is first attributed to Epictus who was a writer around 60 AD! Each of us can experience the same event, but it can have a different meaning, depending on variables such as our age, experience, family background, birth order, health, financial stability, education, personalities and current circumstances. If we look at how we can apply this idea in a book on stress relief for teachers, it follows that some teachers may experience events as stressful, but others see them as exciting and exhilarating. Rather than getting lost in the 'who has most stress?' debate, it makes much more sense to explore the meaning of particular stressors. Over the next few days notice people who talk about 'being stressed'. If it seems appropriate, see if you can shift the focus of the conversations from the stress itself to the particular meaning of the stress. You don't need to come up with a solution – just listen and, as you do, notice if the meaning of that stress is identical for you or different. Notice how simply considering the meaning of the stress or the stressor can distance you a little from the stress or stressor.

Individual differences

We are all different. No one individual through history is credited with that discovery! Yes, we are different, but we are very similar too. As human beings, irrespective of our country of origin, our physiological makeup is similar. The normal expectation when babies are born is that they will each have one head, two eyes, a heart, two lungs and so on. The rate of development will be individual and will depend on external variables such as availability and quality of food and internal factors such as each child's unique genetic coding. The pathway of development will be so similar, however, we can often forget that 'being different' is normal rather than abnormal. Many of us learn at a very young age that it is not alright to be different and we can spend our lives trying to fit in with the norm. Just think of the stress that mission in life inevitably creates! So how is it that some young children learn that they are basically good and worthy, while others learn the opposite? As teachers, we know that many children arrive to school at the ages of four and five believing themselves to be a failure and worthless. Why?

Professor Alan Carr's *The Handbook of Child and Adolescent Clinical Psychology* (Carr, 1999) provides detailed descriptions of the numerous difficulties children can experience in childhood. These include problems of infancy and early childhood such as sleep, toileting, learning and communication difficulties and autism and pervasive developmental disorders; problems of middle childhood such as conduct problems, fear and anxiety problems; and problems in adolescence such as drug abuse and mood problems. Some difficulties such as child abuse can affect children at any stage of their development. It is obviously simplistic and inaccurate to suggest that these and other difficulties arise solely because of the child's ability to learn. Carr (1999) presents a clear summary of how predisposing factors (such as the child's genetic makeup, his attachment with his parents and stresses he may experience early in life) can interact with maintaining factors (coping strategies, family and social supports) and protective factors (health, ability, education) to respond to precipitating factors (such as illness, bullying, or lifecycle transitions) in a way which leads to psychological problems. However, there are so many examples of people 'surviving' extreme adverse circumstances in their early lives it is clear that our approach to life, which is usually learned at a young age, is significant.

Learning theorists

While people throughout time have studied how people learn, and how best to help people learn, the term 'learning theorists' refers mainly to the ideas of Ivan Pavlov (1849–1936) and B.F. Skinner (1903–1990). These men focused on a key question: 'Is behaviour learned or instinctual?' The many contributions of their work are seen in schools and classrooms worldwide. They are also seen in the fields of medicine, of psychology and psychiatry. But perhaps none of those different agents have used learning theory principles as effectively as those who work in marketing. Pavlov's demonstrations of how dogs could be trained to salivate to a bell did not go unnoticed or unforgotten. Wandering through a large department store we can be lulled into a relaxed, almost zombie like state. We may not notice the strategic positioning of signs such as 'For Sale', 'Special Offer' and 'Buy One – Get One Free!'. We may not notice how we have been successfully conditioned to respond to such notices and 'impulse buy'. The chances are, however, that we will gravitate towards these areas and more often than not make a purchase.

Skinner demonstrated how reinforcement, both positive and negative, could be influential in shaping behaviour. It can be a bit upsetting to think that we can 'train' a child to behave in certain ways through rewarding good behaviour and ignoring bad behaviour, in much the same ways that animals such as seals and dolphins can be trained to perform tricks! We can though. If teachers 'reward' children's bad behaviour by giving them attention, we can be certain that they are also reinforcing the same behaviour. Ignoring the bad behaviour and focusing on the positive is essential in helping a child to behave differently.

What have Pavlov and Skinner to do with stress relief? Well, as we have seen, if we learn to react in a certain manner to situations we perceive as stressful we can unlearn and relearn. This might not necessarily be easy, as people who have tried to change their eating habits can testify, but it can be done! Seligman (1992, 1995) identified the powerful impact that reinforcing passive behaviour can have and raised interest in researchers studying 'learned helplessness'. This is certainly not a new concept for teachers. How many of us have felt so frustrated with a particular child because he will not try – 'I can't do it, teacher, I can't.' The exasperated reply 'How do you know you can't if you won't try?' will only be met with a definite 'I just know I can't'. It is all too obvious that positive reinforcement techniques are not enough to convince the child otherwise. Learning is therefore clearly not simply a case of automatic stimulus-response as Pavlov first thought. It involves a much more complex interaction of social and cognitive factors as people such as Bandura, Beck and Ellis have found. We will consider their various contributions after the next section, which presents an overview of the literature on coping with stress.

Coping with stress

The research literature on stress is infinite. The work of Selye (1956, 1974) and Caplan (1964) has been influential in highlighting the links between stress and the physiological response and in focusing attention on the value and importance of prevention. Lazarus developed research interests in how people cope with stress as opposed to who has the most stress and emphasised the importance of perception and appraisal (e.g. Lazarus, 1966; Lazarus and Folkman, 1985). Lazarus defined coping as 'the cognitive and behavioural efforts to manage specific external or internal demands (and conflicts between them) that are appraised as taxing or exceeding the resources of a person' (Lazarus, 1991: 112).

We are all familiar with 'stress questionnaires'. Many of these are developed from the Social Readjustment Rating Scale devised by Holmes and Rahe (1967). Friedman and Rosenman (1974) examined how personality type can influence our ability to cope with stress – and 'Type A' and 'Type B' personality types have now become part of our everyday vocabulary. 'Type A' has been described as having the following characteristics: competitive, verbally aggressive, hard-driving, unable to relax, very time conscious, easily angered and hostile, while 'Type B' is the opposite (Blonna, 1996). However, instead of seeing them as rigid personality types, it is probably more helpful to see them as types of behaviour.

Here is a quick exercise to determine if you are predominantly more prone to use 'Type A' than 'Type B' behaviour. When you are stopped at traffic lights what do you do? Do you use the few seconds to change the radio station, check your hair, find something in the back seat (type B behaviour) or do you keep your foot close by the accelerator, watching carefully for the instant the red light changes to green? Not surprisingly people who are prone to using more 'type A' behaviours have also been found to be at a greater risk of coronary heart disease than those who use 'type B' behaviours (Rosenman and Chesney, 1985).

Kobassa (1979) introduced a third possibility: 'the Hardy' personality, which was someone who was either an A or a B type, but who was resilient. Resilience itself has become a key area of interest in the current stress literature (Rutter, 1985, 1990). Throughout history, and certainly in the past five years, there have been countless examples of children and adults who have been faced with extreme stress. Some of the more resilient of these have managed to cope well, while others who may be more vulnerable do not survive. Dr Erica Frydenberg has built on this work by focusing on the particular elements involved in coping and researching how people can be helped to increase their coping skills (Frydenberg, 1997, 1999).

I first became interested in how people cope with stress in 1986. As part of my studies in psychology I engaged in research examining how teachers, nurses, policemen, managers and owner-managers coped with stress. My sample was very small but the results highlighted for me that people do in fact rely on different ways of coping with stress. I found the measure *Coping Resources Inventory* by Hammer and Marting (1987) extremely helpful and I have often used their five key resources to explain the nature of coping: cognitive, social, emotional, spiritual/philosophical and physical.

Social support as a particular resource, or multidimensional coping strategy, has been studied extensively in coping research. It can be viewed as instrumental support in helping to deal with a problem, concrete support in the form of tangible assistance, or the provisions of emotional support from another. Social support has been deemed to play an increasingly significant role in both the appraisal of stress and the way in which it is managed. It may be used by males and females to manage different problems. The overall weight of evidence from research supports the beneficial effects of social support for well-being as a buffer against stress (Frydenberg, 1999).

O'Connor and Sheehy (2001) emphasised the importance of helping vulnerable people reduce the sense of hopelessness they might feel. Persistence is a key quality that aids successful coping (Dweck, 1998). The effects of persistence may be to facilitate greater effort in finding coping strategies and generating and trying a greater range of strategies. This assists in problem-focused coping particularly. However, it is important to adapt coping to the demands of the situation. In situations where a stressor is incontrollable, the best coping strategy is unlikely to be a problem-focused strategy that results in individual attempts to master the stressor. For example, the use of emotion-focused strategies such as denial, distancing or habituation has been related to better post-war outcomes for children (Muldoon and Cairns, 1999). The ability to understand and communicate emotion in acceptable ways has been identified as a key factor in developing positive relationships (Eisenberg, 1998).

McNamara (2000) has written a comprehensive summary of the various definitions of stress, psychological theories, stressful life events, the role of coping, moderating factors in the stress process and stress-related outcome in her book *Stress in Young People. What's New and What can we Do?*. Her second book *Stress Management Programme for Secondary School Students* (McNamara, 2001) answers her own question 'What can we do?' by providing teachers with a practical, research-based programme to help young people cope with stress. Using stories in a therapeutic way is another tool that can be used to cope with stress (e.g. Hayes, 1999; Meyer, 1996; Divinyi, 1995; Williams, 1995). An excellent book on stress is *Coping with Stress in a Changing World* (Blonna, 1996).

Cognitive and social learning theorists

Learning is a very complex activity. Piaget (1958, 1983) highlighted that intellectual development occurs in stages and that young children are simply not able to grasp certain concepts that come easily to older children. They learn at their own pace and while teachers can help them learn, they cannot force them to do so. In recent years I have assessed numerous children who have some sort of reading difficulties. Many of their parents believe that they are dyslexic (my horror of labels immediately translates this as meaning 'has dyslexia'). Consistently, however, I find that they do not. The vast majority of the children I have assessed for reading difficulties have had an emotional block to reading – somewhere when they were being taught to read they learned that they were 'no good' at reading. This idea became reinforced and quite quickly became a reality. Paradoxically, additional support in school was often the key reinforcer. So how is it that some children learn to become self-confident, while others learn to give up easily? Seligman (1995) has written a wonderful book called *The Optimistic Child* in which he explains how we cannot simply pour self-esteem into children. Instead, self-esteem and a positive self-concept come about as a direct result of our own efforts. As teachers we need to reward for effort much more than for success.

We are continually bombarded with the idea that 'you can if you think you can' and 'you can't if you think you can't'. This is due in a large way to the work of Albert Bandura, Albert Ellis and Aaron Beck. Bandura, a Canadian psychologist born in 1925, researched the effects that observing certain behaviours had on the observers' own behaviour. Perhaps he may not have been the first person to notice how useless the 'do as I say, not what I do' instruction is, but his various research work bears testimony to the inherent truth in that statement. Children very definitely do copy what they see around them – they copy their parents' and teachers' mannerisms, they copy their peers and, worryingly, they copy what they see on television. Bandura developed traditional learning theory ideas to focus on Social Learning Theory. His ideas can be seen in practice in all sorts of training situations where people learn first by observing and then by modelling their behaviour on that of the person they had observed. Bandura is also highly respected for his work on how people learn self-efficacy (Bandura, 1977, 1997). This is based on social learning theory and locus of control theory. It holds that people who believe they exercise genuine control over important factors in their life act in accordance with this belief and feel able to tackle demands on them. Many teachers who feel powerless in their schools to effect change can testify to the stress that creates for them.

Ellis (1913–) is an American clinical psychologist and psychoanalyst. He developed Rational Emotive Behavioural Therapy (REBT), and is considered to be the 'grandfather' of Cognitive Behavioural Therapy (CBT)

(Corey, 1996). Ellis emphasised how we can have irrational beliefs that can cause us great distress. My story of traffic attendants is my way of illustrating just how powerful these beliefs can be. Our body responds as if the belief is true and so if we believe that there is a mouse underneath our chair, and we believe that we are afraid of mice, our body will automatically respond with a fear response. Ellis' work on beliefs explains why the 'you can if you think you can' approach actually does not work! It does not work, because if deep down we actually *believe* we can't do something, we will consciously or unconsciously ensure that that is the case. In fact, repeatedly telling someone that 'you can't because you think you can't' is unfair and completely counter-productive. If changing behaviour was that easy we would all be Olympic gold medallists! Let us suppose that a child in one of your classes is struggling with maths. He believes that he 'can't do it'. Telling him to 'think positively' can actually end up with him feeling even more demoralised, even more certain he can't do it and also blaming himself because he is not thinking the right way about it! Accepting that he actually believes that he can't do it is a different approach. Then you can begin to work with Ellis' idea of 'disputing' his beliefs – gathering concrete evidence about all the things he has done to prove he *can* do things, learn, and succeed. All the things that in actual fact dispute his belief of being useless! Ellis developed an A-B-C-D theory that is central to Rational Emotive Behaviour Therapy. 'A' is the activating event that triggers 'B' the belief to cause 'C' the consequence. The way to break this pattern is by learning to dispute the belief! Dryden (2001) has written a very comprehensive workbook called *Reason to Change: A Rational Emotive Behaviour Therapy (REBT) Workbook* which gives many practical exercises for identifying core beliefs, changing unhealthy ones and strengthening healthy ones. You might also like to look at some of Ellis' own writings, e.g. Ellis (1962, 1993) and Ellis and Harper (1975).

Although Beck is only eight years younger than Ellis he is attributed with being the 'father' of cognitive-behaviour therapy, i.e. how you think affects how you feel affects how you behave. Many practitioners have dropped the 'behaviour' part and see themselves as 'cognitive' therapists, although as far as I am aware, they still actively work with helping people change their behaviour. Beck has made an enormous contribution in scientifically researching his way of working and in demonstrating that CBT works (e.g. Beck, 1963, 1967; Beck *et al.*, 1979). While he originally used it to help people cope with depression, Beck and his colleagues quickly saw its benefits for treating anxiety (e.g. Beck and Emery, 1985). CBT is now used worldwide to help people cope with practically any difficulty. Weishaar (1993) has written a very interesting account of Beck and the contribution and influence of his therapy. A comprehensive list of books in cognitive-behavioural therapy as well as details of numerous research articles can be found in the website of the Beck Institute, i.e. http://www.beckinstitute.org/index.html.

The 'Coping Triangle' is my way of presenting the key principles of CBT. Beck tends to use a more traditional format of columns and of helping people rate the way they feel and the extent to which they believe their thoughts as well as helping them to generate different thoughts. He noted that people with depression tend to have a 'negative triad', i.e. a negative view about themselves, their world and their future, and he worked to help people confront this and change it. Beck built on the ideas of Donald Meichenbaum who illustrated the benefits of helping people to become more aware of their self-talk (Meichenbaum, 1977, 1986). He then helped people to classify their thoughts as 'positive' and 'negative'. In the 'Coping Triangle' I have adapted that to classify thoughts as 'helpful' and 'unhelpful'.

I had the privilege of visiting Beck's clinic in Philadelphia in 1996 and observed him working with a young man who had a long history of severe depression. CBT differs from Rogers' *Client-Centered Therapy* (Rogers, 1951, 1980, 1986) in that it is 'directional' as opposed to 'non-directional'. However, observing Beck made me realise just how much he shared Rogers' emphasis on 'unconditional positive regard' for his client. Even though I was sitting in a different room watching the session through a video camera, the depth of Beck's utmost respect and regard for the young man before him was so obvious. He very gently helped him identify the thoughts he had which kept him 'stuck' and made socialising enormously difficult for him. His next step was to help the client to identify particular activities he would like to do but felt unable to do so. The final step in the session was to work with him in designing practical tasks that would help him work towards changing his behaviour so as to ultimately help him feel better.

Watching the session I was struck very forcibly by how simple Beck made his therapy seem. Was it actually that easy, or was it more that I was watching a Master at work? I think really it is a bit of both. The basics of CBT are common sense. We cannot, however, impose these basic ideas on anyone, as to do so would discount the personal meaning for the individual of the particular difficulties he/she is experiencing! It can be very damaging, as well as completely disrespectful, to 'help' someone by telling them that their current situation is their own fault, because they are thinking the wrong way and doing the wrong things! I see the various techniques of CBT as 'tools of the trade'. Their effectiveness depends primarily on how they are used! Just as a hammer is a dangerous weapon in the hands of an unskilled tradesman, CBT cannot be just shown to someone. Looking back I think the session I observed with Beck and his client looked easy *because* Beck was so skilled and caring.

Perhaps now is a good time to emphasise again that the ideas in this book are intended to be a way of introducing the core CBT principles to teachers as a means of helping them make sense of their stress and to help them relieve it. It is not in any way intended to be a replacement for therapy, or a way of creating amateur therapists!

Cognitive-behavioural therapy with children

Professor Philip Kendall is recognised worldwide for his work in using CBT with children, both as a form of treatment, and as a means of prevention. I first met Professor Kendall in the summer of 1993 when I was mid-way through my clinical psychology training. I had a very strong 'ha-ha' reaction as I sat in the middle of a large group at a workshop he was running. He started his presentation by showing us all slides of where he went to school, where he went on his holidays and where he worked. The slide show went on for about twenty minutes and towards the end of it a certain amount of people had begun to shuffle in their seats. Professor Kendall then stopped and asked us all to focus on what we were thinking. He suggested that some people might have wondered why they had paid money to see slides they had no interest in and were beginning to feel angry. Others, he pointed out, might have been distracted thinking if there was going to be a break for coffee. Some other people who had been to some of the places shown on the slide might have begun to think of their own experiences there. His key point was that our thoughts were shaped by our own perceptions of his behaviour and their subsequent reactions, that they were very powerful and were also linked to our feelings. I was hooked!!! Two years later Professor Kendall invited me to do some training with him in Philadelphia. He is a meticulous researcher, and another clinician whose major strength is how he uses his 'tools of the trade' in a respectful, caring way.

One of the essential features of CBT in children is to help the child to identify dysfunctional cognitions and to become aware of its impact on thinking and subsequent behaviour (Kendall *et al.*, 1997). Other identified strategies include exposure, use of relaxation techniques and modelling (Labellarte *et al.*, 1999). Beneficial therapy effects are associated with three main factors: 1 use of behavioural and cognitive-behavioural strategies; 2 reliance of specific focused therapy methods rather than missed or eclectic ones; and 3 provision of guidelines for treatment such as treatment manuals and careful monitoring of the treatment process to ensure adherence to those treatment guidelines (Wiesz *et al.*, 1995). Cognitive-behavioural strategies use active procedures as well as cognitive interventions to produce changes in thinking, feelings and behaviour (Kendall, 1992; Friedberg, 1996; Weist and Danforth, 1998).

CBT is an easier therapy to research and evaluate than many other therapies because it can be 'standardised' in the form of a treatment manual. Critics of this approach have warned that this ignores the individual needs of clients. Professor Kendall's view, which I share, is that CBT manuals should be used creatively by the therapist to best help the particular needs of the individual (Kendall *et al.*, 1998). Professor Kendall's 'Coping Cat' treatment programme (Kendall, 1992) has been used very successfully to help children cope with anxiety (e.g. Kendall, 1994, 1998; Kendall and Southam-Gerow, 1996; Kendall and Flannery-Schroeder, 1998).

The 'Coping Cat' has been adapted very successfully in Australia where it has become the 'Coping Koala' and used as part of the 'Friends' programmes. Dr Paula Barrett and her team have the results of numerous research studies to testify to the effectiveness of manualised cognitive-behavioural treatment programmes for individual children as well as for families (Barrett *et al.*, 2001; Barrett *et al.*, 1996). In the Netherlands Dr Maaike Nauta has demonstrated the effectiveness of using cognitive-behavioural therapy to treat anxiety disorders in children and adolescents (Nauta, 2005). Cognitive-behavioural group treatments have also been found to be very beneficial for working with children who have depression (Lewinsohn *et al.*, 1990; Lewinsohn *et al.*, 1996; Dwivedi and Varma, 1997; Lewinsohn and Clarke, 1999).

Prevention using cognitive-behavioural principles

In recent years attention has turned to examining how CBT principles can be used in a preventative way. From 1998 to 2000 I was a therapist in the ODIN European research into preventing depression in adults using a psychoeducational cognitive-behavioural programme, *The Coping with Depression Course* (Lewinsohn *et al.*, 1984). The results of this research are very positive and encouraging (e.g. Dowrick *et al.*, 2000). I was amazed by how much I personally benefited from my involvement in the research. I found that automatically I became much more aware of my thoughts and while often being shocked at how harsh I was towards myself, I was able to change my actions in a helpful way. Many of the adults I worked with in the various groups told me how sorry they were that they had not learned these simple, basic, but highly effective, ideas years before. They reinforced my own view that the basic principles of CBT should be taught as a matter of course in schools.

From 1997 I worked with Dr Mark Morgan, seven guidance counsellors, and over 700 twelve/thirteen-year-olds to determine if adolescents felt that they needed help in coping and if so, if a group psychoeducational programme could help them cope. This became the basis for my doctoral research, which was funded by the Irish Department of Education and Science. The results demonstrated how a psychoeducational programme 'The Helping Adolescents Cope Programme' adapted, with permission, from Albano *et al.* (1997) was effective in reducing depression in young adolescents and increasing their ability to cope (Hayes and Morgan, 2005; Hayes, 2001a, 2001b).

Examples of how diverse psychoeducational programmes have become include: helping young people at risk of dropping out of school prematurely (Christenson and Brooke Carroll, 1999); changing young people's explanatory style from pessimism to optimism (Seligman, 1995); coping with sexual transitions (Morgan, 2000; Moore *et al.*, 1995; Moore, 1999); treating bullying (Olweous, 1994); preventing sexual abuse (MacIntyre and Lawlor, 1991; MacIntyre and Carr, 1999); normalising eating behaviour (Braet, 1999); treating conduct disorders (Waddell *et al.*, 1999); preventing substance abuse (Morgan *et al.*, 1996; Rollin *et al.*, 1999); preventing teenage pregnancy (Nitz, 1999); treating anxiety (Kendall, 1993, 1994; Kendall and Southam-Gerow, 1996; Stark and Kendall, 1996); preventing depression (Reynolds and Coates, 1986; Clarke *et al.*, 1990; Lewinsohn *et al.*, 1990; Stark *et al.*, 1991; Jaycock *et al.*, 1994; Rice and Meyer, 1994; Clarke *et al.*, 1995; Stark and Smith, 1995; Cuijpers, 1998; Seligman *et al.*, 1999).

While psychoeducational programmes have been found to be of great value, they are not a panacea. For example, some researchers question the ethics of suicide psychoeducational prevention programmes. Most such programmes employ a stress model of suicide, as opposed to a mental illness model. Suicide is presented as a reaction to extreme psychosocial or interpersonal stress and the link to mental illness is markedly de-emphasised (Diekstra *et al.*, 1995). There researchers were concerned that 'in their attempts to "destigmatise" suicide some school-based suicide prevention programmes may be normalising the behaviour and reducing potentially protective taboos' (p. 735).

It is also important to recognise the enormous pressure teachers are under. The argument for placing mental health services in schools is that it will increase access to services and increase the likelihood that these will reach those in need and promote the chances of educational success (Ghuman and Sarles, 1998; Weissberg and Greenberg, 1998). Others such as Coolahan (2000) refer to the increasing pressure being placed on the school to compensate for some of the difficulties of society. The World Health Organisation is among those who see schools as having much to contribute to mental health. As a move to encourage schools to be more mental health promoting, it has formulated nine steps to becoming 'child friendly' as an integral part of the school curriculum (World Health Organisation, 1997). While schools alone cannot change whole communities, researchers stress that they are in a unique position to initiate and lead effective prevention efforts in a community (Tinzmann and Hikson, 1992; Head, 1997; Weist, 1998; Dornbusch *et al.*, 1999; Frydenberg, 1999).

An unexpected long-term finding of the 'Helping Adolescents Cope' research was that not one of the seven guidance counsellors who had been involved in the research implemented the programme again. This was surprising and disappointing, as each of them was so definite that the programme had been highly effective. When I explored this further I discovered that while they saw the definite benefits in working in a preventative way, they did not have the time or the resources to do so, outside the structure of a research project. I later discovered from some colleagues in Australia and the Netherlands that this is not unique to Ireland. The school day is so busy and the school curriculum is so packed that there can be very little real space for prevention work. I decided to introduce the basics of CBT to teachers in a different way – hence the 'Coping Triangle' and this book!

Over the past two years I have used the 'Coping Triangle' in a clinical setting with adults and children. Generally over five sessions I help people make sense of their distress, learn the nature of anxiety and depression and examine how their thoughts and actions affect their feelings: a key element as they begin to identify how unhelpful many of their thoughts are to help them develop compassion towards themselves, as has been recommended by Gilbert (2005). It is very gratifying to see how applying the 'Coping Triangle' works so quickly. I always emphasise that 'action' is the key – we may understand the connection between our thoughts, actions and feelings, but if we continue to blame, terrify or harm ourselves by unhelpful actions, it is more difficult for us to actually feel better. The challenge is not waiting until we do feel better before we start doing 'helpful' things! To adapt the title of Susan Jeffers book slightly: 'Feel the feeling, but do it anyway!'

Helpful actions might include consulting a GP or a Consultant for medical advice; taking prescribed medication; reading helpful material; working with a therapist; obtaining social support at work; practising meditation or yoga, increasing the amount and quality of pleasurable activities and generally giving ourselves permission to 'just be'. While I firmly believe in the benefits of a CBT approach to understanding difficulties, and in learning to cope with them, there are many other effective approaches, which I see as complementing CBT approaches as opposed to being alternatives. Kedar Nath Dwivedi and Peter Brinley Harper are the editors of a book *Promoting the Emotional Well-being of Children and Adolescents and Preventing Their Mental Ill Health* (Dwivedi and Brinley Harper, 2004). This addresses a wide range of topics including parenting (Waldsax, 2004), life skills education through schools (Coley and Dwivedi, 2004), preventing depression and anxiety (Hayes, 2004), preventing eating disorders (Stewart, 2004), and ethnic minority children and families and mental health (Messent, 2004).

Learning more about cognitive-behavioural approaches to coping

Since Beck first began developing, researching and publishing his ideas, many others have done the same. There is now a vast array of books written by well-respected professionals to introduce the key CBT principles to the general public in the form of 'self-help' books. I strongly recommend that you look up the following website address just to see the range and scale of some of these: http://www.cognitivetherapy.com/books.html

Dr David Burns wrote a book in 1980 that became an international best seller – *Feeling Good: The New Mood Therapy*. It is one of the key books I recommend to people, as well as his follow-up book *The Feeling Good Handbook* (Burns, 1989) and *Ten Days to Great Self-Esteem* (Burns, 1999). Dr Tony Bates worked with Beck and Burns and his book *Depression: The Commonsense Approach* (Bates, 1999) is very clear, practical and helpful. I recommend that book as a matter of course to all of my clients. His chapter on CBT in an earlier book *Psychotherapy in Ireland* (Bates, 1993) provides a concise summary of the theory of CBT and how it can be applied in practice.

The Warneford Hospital in Oxford has become recognised as a Specialist Centre for Cognitive Therapy. They run training courses and details of these are available on the following website: http://www.rdlearning. org.uk/CourseDetails.asp?ID=24203. Many of the team have written excellent books, which I strongly recommend. These include: *Manage Your Mind* (Butler and Hope, 1998); *Overcoming Social Anxiety: A Self-help Guide Using Cognitive Behavioural Techniques* (Butler, 1999); *Overcoming Low Self-esteem: Self-help Guide Using Cognitive Behavioural Techniques* (Fennell, 1999); and *Overcoming Anxiety: A Self-help Guide to Using Cognitive Behavioural Techniques* (Kennerley, 1997). The psychologists working in the Warneford Hospital have also published information booklets for the general public on a wide range of conditions. A list of these can be found on the following website: http://www.octc.co.uk/html/body_self-help.html. Four other self-help books I strongly recommend are: *Overcoming Depression: A Self-help Guide Using Cognitive Behavioural Techniques* (Gilbert, 2000); *The Anxiety and Phobia Workbook* (Bourne, 2000); *Self-Esteem: A Proven Program of Cognitive Techniques for Assessing, Improving and Maintaining Your Self-Esteem* (McKay and Fanning, 2000); and *Mind over Mood* (Greenberger and Padesky, 1995). Useful books for school guidance counsellors are *Think Good – Feel Good: A Cognitive Behaviour Therapy Workbook for Children and Young People* by Stallard (2002) and *Cognitive-behaviour Therapy for Children and Families* (Graham, 1998). An article by Friedberg (1996) gives some very useful suggestions on cognitive-behavioural games and workbooks for school counsellors. You might also like to look at Byron Katie's website where she gives details of *The Work* – an approach designed to help people challenge their thoughts (www.thework.org). Finally, I have always found any of Gael Lindenfield's books very easy to read and full of common sense, e.g. *Positive under Pressure* (Lindenfield and Vanderburg, 2000) and *Self-esteem* (Lindenfield, 2000).

Stress and the teacher

As you were reading the various paragraphs in this chapter did you wonder why I had not prioritised the whole area of teachers and stress? Why I had not listed the causes of stress for teachers and reported on key research findings to illustrate how to cope with it? Yes, there is a vast amount of evidence demonstrating that teaching can be a very stressful occupation. Jarvis (2002) in his critical review of recent findings on teacher stress highlights three broad causal factors for this: 1 factors intrinsic to teaching, 2 cognitive factors affecting the individual vulnerability of teachers, and 3 systemic factors operating at the institutional and political level. There is universal recognition among teachers and researchers alike that classroom discipline is a very definite stressor (e.g. Lewis, 1999; Martin, 1997; Hart *et al.,* 1995). Other factors intrinsic to teaching have included work overload (Pithers and Soden, 1998; Travers and Cooper, 1997), low pay (Jarvis, 2002) and the pressure on teachers for their students to perform well in state examinations (Martin, 1997). Systemic factors such as lack of support, the role of parents and societal changes can be influential in teachers 'burning out' from too much stress and/or from difficulties in coping with it (Kyriacou, 2001).

As you may have guessed, my interest in 'stress and teaching' focuses primarily on teachers' individual reactions to the various stressors they face as well as their ability to cope with them. Jarvis (2002) points out that while there has been a substantial volume of research into the causes of teacher stress, there has been little work done on research around how to reduce or mediate this stress. He suggests that given the cognitive factors affecting teachers' susceptibility to stress, CBT-based interventions might be effective.

The 'Coping Triangle' is my way of introducing the key CBT principles to teachers as a means of relieving their stress. I am aware that it may not change many stressors, but my hope is that it will help change your perception towards it and, in so doing, relieve stress. The following chapter presents three key stressors: disclosure of abuse by a student; a student who is seriously ill; and student disinterest, and looks at how you might use the 'Coping Triangle' to help you identify your own individual response in terms of your thoughts, feelings and actions and use these to help you cope effectively. My hope is that this overview of the theory underpinning the 'Coping Triangle' will encourage you to read further. So, now – from theory to practice!

9 From theory to practice!

Do you remember Exercise 7.2, which was at the end of Chapter 7? I suggested that you might apply the 'Coping Triangle' to help one of your colleagues who is considering leaving teaching altogether. Briefly the story went as follows: he reacted very aggressively to another teacher in a staff meeting, refused to apologise, later announced he was giving up teaching. Then when you meet him for a coffee you realise that he has very serious worries about his wife's health and the effect that is having on his two young children. Have a look at the suggested approach below and see how it compares with your own response.

Suggested approach to helping friend relieve stress

1   Listen, without judgement and without interrupting. Become aware of your own thoughts and feelings and your initial reaction to reassure, rescue or respect his ability to reflect on the day and learn from it. If your friend is clear that he does not want you to help him it is important that you respect his wishes. 'Helping Messiahs' are actually not helpful (for proof read Berry, 1988, 1991; Hayes, 2000). However, if he is open to your sharing some stress relief strategies with him you might proceed as listed below.
2   What is the initial meaning of the Physical Education teacher's comment for you and for your colleague?
3   Use the 'Stress Equation' to list the various stressors your friend is under as well as establishing his own perception of these stressors and the level of external support he is receiving.
4   Use the metaphor of the 'Volcano' to illustrate how logical it is that he would have erupted in the school staff-room if he has buried his feelings over a long period of time.
5   Use the 'Coping Triangle' to help him identify his feelings, thoughts and actions before, during and after the 'explosion' at the meeting.
6   If he might have thoughts such as 'he should be able to cope without help' – 'he has let everyone down' – 'he has made a complete fool of himself', etc. gently wonder if these thoughts might be due to some

underlying core beliefs such as 'it is weak to need help'. Tell him the story of the Traffic Attendants and remind him that though people believed that the world was flat, it is in fact round!

7   Teach him the basic tenets of the 'Coping Triangle' – i.e. it is not the event, but the meaning of the event, that causes stress. Thoughts affect feelings affect actions. Scary thoughts are generally unhelpful and lead to feelings of anxiety and fear. Harsh judgemental thoughts are also generally unhelpful and lead to shame and guilt. Both types of thoughts frequently lead to unhelpful actions.

8   Explore the impact of all of this on him by asking him to define himself in terms of 'I am . . .' Ask him if he really, 100 per cent believes that he is in fact . . .

9   Help him focus on his actions. List all the helpful actions he does on a daily basis – actions he may probably dismiss and/or minimise such as dressing and feeding the children, making the meals, getting to work, standing in the classroom, etc. Help him see how little credit he gives himself for his achievements in contrast to the harsh criticism he throws at himself when he fails to meet his demanding, unfair and often unrealistic standards!

10 Focus on as many helpful actions he can take as possible. These might include explaining his home situation to his School Principal; asking some other family member to look after the children for a week; remembering to breathe in slowly while clenching his fist, hold the breath, and then relax his hand as he breathes out; arranging some time off; deliberately planning one 'fun thing' to do everyday with his wife (e.g. going for a walk, a trip to the cinema, meeting for lunch); meeting with his wife's doctors or writing to them to clarify specific medical questions he has. He might also consider if professional support from a therapist or a counsellor would be helpful.

11 Teach him about the 'Coping Sentence' and help him come up with a 'but' response that is true, strong and applicable in many situations. Make sure to put in the words 'I think' after the word 'because'! Some possibilities might include:
'I feel embarrassed because I think I made a complete fool of myself today *but maybe I didn't!*'
'I feel guilty because I think I am not doing enough for my wife, children, students *but I choose to let myself off the hook!*'
'I feel terrified because I think about the future without my wife *but I have no room in my head for those type of thoughts!*'
'I feel ashamed because I think I reacted so badly in the staff meeting today *but I choose to let myself off the hook and apologise tomorrow!*'

12 Revisit the meaning of all of this with your friend. My guess is he would see his stress as being completely ridiculous and a sign of weakness. Look again at his Stress Equation. Given the various stressors he is under (big and small) it is actually much more hopeful

and healthy that he exploded in the staff-room as he did. How much longer could he have continued to bottle up his feelings? How much long-term damage would that do?

13   Finally, reflect on the meaning of all of this for you. It can feel very satisfying to help someone make sense of their stress and to help them to cope. It can also be very daunting – and timing is everything!

You might wonder why I have asked you to apply the various techniques in this book to help someone else relieve his stress, rather than focus on your own. The answer is simple – it is generally easier to be positive and see solutions for somebody else. We can too easily become overwhelmed and hopeless when we are faced with our own challenges. I must caution, however, about the 'Helping Messiah' phenomenon. I referred to it above in passing, as I did not want to interrupt the sequence of steps, but *When Helping You is Hurting Me. Escaping the Messiah Trap* (Berry, 1988) and *How to Escape the Messiah Trap. A Workbook for When Helping You is Hurting Me* (Berry, 1991) are two very important books. Unfortunately they are out of print, but you might be able to track them down through your local library or on the Internet. Alternatively you might be interested in reading my own personal review of both books (Hayes, 2000). Basically Berry cautions against people becoming addicted to helping, and then like any addict seeking out supplies for their 'fix'. Developing a dependency on 'helping needy people', she explains, can be as destructive as dependencies on other more obvious things, such as substances. She points out the double-sided trap of helping: 'If I don't do it, it won't get done', and 'Everyone else's needs come before mine', and illustrates how this trap actually hurts the people we are trying to help, as well as ourselves. Berry describes seven distinct types of 'The Helping Messiah', i.e. the Pleaser, the Rescuer, the Giver, the Counsellor, the Protector, the Teacher and the Crusader. She explains that the teacher Messiahs are unique from the others as they try to help people in groups. She cautions that they are motivated by a deep need for approval and can find saying 'no' almost impossible. You might not be too surprised to hear that they may find it impossible to share their own vulnerabilities and acknowledge failings. Sadly it is so true that 'teachers can be surrounded by people and yet agonizingly alone' (Berry, 1988: 54).

So, now, for a moment consider your role in the staff-room – are you the person who watches out for the new teachers to give them extra support? Do you tend to agree for the sake of keeping the peace and often wish that others would do the same? Do you go home cringing that you allowed people to 'walk all over you'? Do you find yourself enjoying the 'helping' side of your job most and notice that you have loose professional boundaries with the students who seem most in need? As you have been reading this book have you thought (even once!) 'I know who should read this book – it might help her cope with the stress she is under'?

If you have answered 'yes' to even one of these questions I would strongly encourage you to read Berry's books. 'Helping' when we choose to do so is vital – 'helping' because we cannot say 'no', or because we cannot allow someone else the space to come to his own solution, or because we will feel 'bad' if we don't help, or because 'we love being needed' is completely and totally wrong! So, do you want to revise your steps in helping your colleague?

The next three exercises are aimed at helping you use the 'Coping Triangle' to help you cope with three very different situations – being told by a student that she is being abused; teaching a student who is severely ill; and teaching students who just do not want to learn. As you read through the exercises, notice your thoughts, your feelings and your actions.

Exercise 9.1

Situation: One of your students has hung back after class and has asked you to keep a secret. Without thinking you agree and are then horrified to hear her tell you that she is being abused. She is upset and will not tell you who the alleged perpetrator is or the exact nature of the abuse. At this point take a few moments to complete the 'Coping Triangle' in Exercise 9.1 below.

Exercise 9.1 'Coping Triangle': Hearing story of abuse

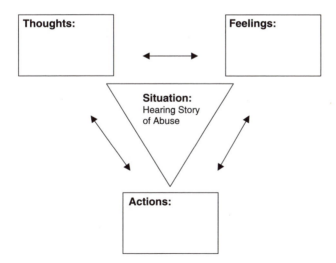

The chances are that in that situation you might feel upset, worried, unsure. What does the student's story mean to you? It is almost impossible to get accurate statistics for abuse as definitions vary widely. However, if we take a conservative figure that one in ten people may be victims of abuse, it follows that you also may be a victim of abuse. In that case it is obvious that the meaning for you will be totally different from the meaning for someone who has not had that experience. If this is the case you may experience feelings of intense anger. Ask yourself: 'Do my feelings make sense?' If they do, acknowledge how difficult and upsetting this may be for you and move to look at your thoughts. Of course, if you have never had any experience in this area you may feel curious and perhaps proud that the student chose you to confide in.

You may have listed some of the following thoughts:

- Oh, no, I don't believe it.
- The poor girl!
- What do I do?
- I don't want to hear this.
- What if she is lying?
- I wonder who it is.

Check to see if your thoughts are 'helpful' or 'unhelpful'. If you are aware that you have experience of having been abused yourself, be particularly gentle and compassionate with yourself.

As we have seen throughout this book being gentle with our feelings, ignoring our 'unhelpful' thoughts and acting in a helpful way is the key to strong coping. So what might 'helpful' actions be in this situation? You may know already that a golden rule with students is that you never, never, never guarantee complete confidentiality. This can be a very difficult concept for teachers. I have heard the argument 'If I don't promise to keep her secret, then she won't tell me' and 'What is the point of her telling me if I am not going to do something helpful?' Keeping her secret is very definitely not helpful. It places you in a very dangerous position legally, but apart from that, it is very unfair to the student, as your knowing, but doing nothing, is not going to make the abuse stop. My strong advice, based on working for two years in a Child Sexual Abuse Assessment unit, is never, never, never guarantee complete confidentiality. It is so much fairer and more respectful to the student if you say very clearly when you are asked to keep a secret something like: 'Well, I can keep some things secret, but if you tell me that you have seriously hurt someone, or that someone has seriously hurt you, then I have to tell.' In many parts of the world, teachers, like other professionals, are mandated by law to report incidences of abuse to the appropriate authorities. In countries where reporting of child abuse is not mandated, there are generally very definite professional guidelines which teachers are expected to follow. If you guarantee to a student that you will keep a secret, and then tell the authorities, you are betraying her confidence and breaking her trust. It is so much fairer and more respectful if she is aware from the start that telling you is going to lead to you telling someone else. 'But,' you may think, 'what if I tell her that, and then she chooses not to tell me?' Yes, that is a possibility, and in that case I would strongly advise you to report the situation to your School Principal anyway.

I have worked with teachers who see it as part of their role to establish as far as possible that the story they hear is the truth. They have told me that they do not want to 'waste the Principal's time' or 'look stupid' for passing on information that is later found to be untrue. Verifying accounts of child abuse is not part of the teacher's role. I believe it is not part of the school counsellor's role either. Different countries have different ways of proceeding once an allegation of abuse is made, but it is very important that teachers act within the limits of what they are required to do. It may be that the child's story that 'only' this happened and 'no more' is accurate, but perhaps her account is just the tip of the iceberg. Yes, perhaps she is lying, or misinterpreting, but it is not your job as her teacher to verify her account.

The most 'helpful' action in this situation is to tell the child you are sorry that you promised to keep her secret, but you had not realised that she would tell you she was being hurt by someone and that you are obliged to tell the School Principal. Be prepared for her being upset, lashing out at you in anger, and perhaps accusing you of letting her down. Comments such as 'I thought I could trust you, but I can't' can be deeply wounding. It is understandable that the teacher in question will take the comments personally and feel hurt. Using the 'Coping Triangle' ask yourself 'Does it make sense that I feel hurt, when I think that I have let the student down?' The obvious answer is 'yes' as most if not all teachers like to feel trusted by their students. Feeling hurt though is not a good enough reason not to pass on the student's story in line with your school's policy on abuse. My suggestion is that you repeat this 'Coping Sentence' to yourself:

> I feel upset, because I promised to keep that secret and she is upset with me *but I am obliged to pass on all reports of abuse to the School Principal.*

If you are the School Principal you will be familiar with the next step. The idea that children can be abused is horrible. The reality is a million times more so. Having worked in a child sexual abuse assessment unit I am very aware of the need for professional support. Hearing children tell you how they have been hurt by older children and/or adults can be deeply upsetting. I have direct experience of supporting teachers who crossed over their professional boundaries and became too involved with families. Many of them were unprepared for the sheer intensity of emotion children and their families experienced as a result of abuse. It can be tempting to blame ourselves saying: 'If I had kept the child's secret like she asked me to, she would not have to experience the horror of court, or of not being believed, or . . .'

What 'helpful' actions are possible in this scenario? I would strongly recommend that all teachers prepare themselves for this situation by knowing the signs of abuse as well as the specific School Policy on reporting allegations of abuse. It is very important that teachers get professional support around reporting the allegation, particularly, as is often the case, the child's world seems to become more difficult as a result. I strongly advise you to find out the specific guidelines on Child Abuse in your country. You might also like to read the following documents: *Putting Children First: A Discussion Document on Mandatory Reporting of Child Abuse* (Ireland, 1996); *Children First: National Guidelines for the Protection and Welfare of Children* (Ireland, 1999); *Child Protection – Guidelines and Procedures* (Ireland, 2001); and *Child Protection Guidelines for Post-Primary Schools* (Ireland, 2004).

If you feel that you are over-identifying with students and/or find it difficult to keep professional boundaries I strongly encourage you to consider personal counselling/therapy. You cannot be your students' 'best friend' – for their sakes, just as much as for yours!

Exercise 9.2

Situation: It is the start of the school year and you have just found out that one of your students was diagnosed with a serious, possibly life-threatening illness over the summer holidays. As before please take a few moments to complete the 'Coping Triangle' below.

Exercise 9.2 'Coping Triangle': Hearing of student's illness

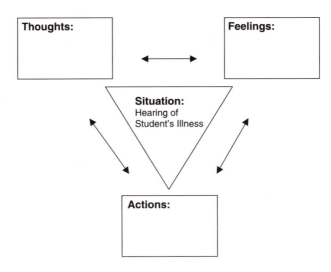

Do your feelings make sense? Are your thoughts 'helpful' or 'unhelpful'? Are your actions 'helpful' or 'unhelpful'? You may feel so upset for the student. If you have personal experience of having had a serious illness yourself, you may notice yourself reflecting on your own experience. If you have recently experienced the death of someone close you may think 'I don't think I can face that again so soon'. You may decide to treat him exactly the same as the others, or you might make a decision that you will not add to his stress in any way and will not expect the same standards from him as before. Take some time with this exercise. As we have seen, your feelings more than likely make sense, given what you are thinking and doing. However, it is vital that you separate out your feelings and experiences from what might be helpful for your student. My experience of working in Children's Hospitals as a teacher, and some years later, as a clinical psychologist, taught me that school can become a real life-line. Serious illness can be terrifying for children and their families. So many things are unknown and far removed from their normal day-to-day life. You may never know the effort it takes a child who is ill to get to school. Often getting there is such an achievement, he is likely to want to forget about his illness for a while. He wants to feel 'normal'. Very few children like to be treated differently from their class-mates. It can be hugely important for him that you continue to expect him to participate in class and give him homework – the meaning for him if you don't might be that you have given up on him having a future and see no point in giving him homework. You might protest and say that you do not want to cause him additional pressure. You might be wrong.

In this case 'helpful actions' might include asking the School Principal and guidance counsellor if there is a School Policy on children with a serious disease. If not, it might be a good time to write one. That will force the staff as a group to confront their own fears around teaching children with an illness, as well as managing practical issues such as how to manage a child's stay in hospital, who is to be the key link with his parents, and what support structures are in place for helping children and teachers in the event of the child dying.

Other helpful actions might include reading about the child's disease or illness so that you have some understanding of what he is experiencing and the implications of that for his continuing to attend school. I would strongly encourage all teachers to read Judy Tatlebaum's gentle book *The Courage to Grieve* (Tatlebaum, 1997) before they are faced with the serious illness and possible death of a student. I also recommend *On Death: Helping Children Understand and Cope* (Smilansky, 1987); *Helping Children Cope with Death: Guidelines and Resources* (Wass and Corr, 1982); *Living with Grief. Children,*

Adolescents and Loss (Doka, 2000); *When a Friend Dies* (Gootman, 1994); *When Someone Very Special Dies. Children can Learn to Cope with Grief* (Heegard, 1991); *On Children and Death* (Kubler-Ross, 1983); and *Death and Loss. Compassionate Approaches in the Classroom* (Leaman, 1995).

Most schools have policies to help them clarify how to respond appropriately when a student dies. It is important that all staff members are clear on the various steps and follow them. Many students who are seriously ill recover. For some they may have physical reminders of how ill they were, e.g. if they had a limb removed and/or are confined to a wheel chair. It can be difficult for them to 'mourn' the loss of the life they had as they might feel that they are 'supposed' to celebrate the fact that they are alive. I would suggest that you as teacher take your cue from your student – rather than assuming you know the meaning of being back in school, of getting homework, or not getting homework, etc. ask him – but at a time when the other students do not hear. Again, it is vital that you as a teacher know the limits of your professional boundaries and stay inside them. Your student might not appreciate your visiting him in hospital or at home – even if it does make you 'feel good' for doing so! My advice is that you follow the School Policy, which ideally will have been discussed with the student's parents in advance, so that there is no ambiguity around visits, cards, drawing attention to the illness in front of the other students, or ignoring it altogether, if that is deemed to be appropriate.

Students will experience other losses – the tragic death of a family member or friend; the ending of their parents' relationships for example. Using the 'Coping Triangle' can help you separate out your feelings and thoughts, so as to be able to focus on acting in a helpful and professional manner.

A possible 'Coping Sentence' for this situation might be:

> I feel anxious, because I do not think I could cope if a student of mine died *but I choose to teach him as well as I can and get additional support if I need it.*

Exercise 9.3

Situation: You are standing in front of your class when you realise that the majority of the students are not interested in what you have to say, are not paying attention and are being deliberately obstructive.

Step One: Complete the 'Coping Triangle' in Exercise 9.3.

Exercise 9.3 'Coping Triangle': Teaching students who do not want to learn

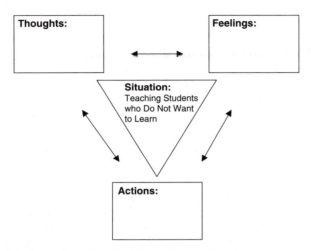

It is possible that when faced with students who do not want to learn you feel exasperated, demoralised, angry, frustrated, upset, and/or hopeless. Just put those feelings to one side for a moment and look at how you are thinking and what you are doing. My guess is that you are blaming either yourself or your students or both. Perhaps you are thinking that you would be better to move to a different school or to give up teaching altogether. Take a few moments to look at what your underlying beliefs might be. Do you believe, really believe, that you are a good teacher? Do you believe that the Principal thinks highly of you? Do you believe that the students enjoy your classes and that their parents think highly of your work? If you are confident of your ability as a teacher and you are feeling as you do because the students are not interested in learning, perhaps it is time that you shifted the focus from how 'they make you feel' to 'what you can do differently'. You might say 'Oh, but I have tried everything – nothing will work'. It is possible that your students might think that you don't enjoy teaching them anyway. Take a moment to choose one student in that class and complete the 'Coping Triangle' as if you were he. You might be surprised to realise how influential your attitude to your students is. If you believe that they are not going to be interested in your class, the chances are you are going to be correct!

Consider all the 'helpful actions' you might take in relieving your stress with these students. They might include some of the following: relaxing with the students, looking for something positive about them and their way of learning; seeking good professional support from a trusted colleague; talking to some of the students individually and encouraging them.

If all else fails, perhaps the most helpful action for you would be to consider moving to another school or changing career altogether. If you decide to do this, take some time to explore the meaning of this for you – are you considering a move because you have 'failed' or because you recognise that at this point in time you would be happier elsewhere and you have very bravely chosen to act on that?

You might think at this point 'Is that it? I have read this book to help me relieve my stress brought on by teaching students who do not want to learn in the first place and I am told to examine my own attitude, thoughts and beliefs, look closely at what I do and if I feel that nothing is going to change, to move?'

If you can sum up this book in that way I would be delighted. Knowing how to relieve stress is not hard – putting the various steps into practice can be much more difficult. You might like to complete another 'Coping Triangle' to explore further why this might be, but at this point I would suggest it is simply because change is often difficult. It may seem easier in some ways to blame the students for not keeping quiet, than to look at how we are contributing to the overall atmosphere in the classroom.

To conclude this chapter I suggest the following 'Coping Sentence':

> I feel annoyed, frustrated, etc. because I think that the students in this class do not want to be here and I am allowing them to drive me mad *but I am the adult and the teacher in the classroom.*

10 Conclusion

Now that you have almost finished this book I wonder if you are more accepting of your own feelings of stress. I hope so. Discovering that you are feeling upset, exhausted, disappointed, demoralised or even attacked at any particular moment in your career is not surprising. Teaching is a tough job. Society expects and indeed demands so much of teachers and yet often seems unwilling to support them in delivering these demands. In fact students can now publicly slander and humiliate their teachers anonymously through use of the Internet. On a good day most teachers will not care what a student or parent writes about them. They will be able to keep a sense of perspective and realise that being 'popular' with students does not necessarily equate with good teaching. However, what about the days when we are not feeling great? The days when we wonder if teaching really is for us? The days when we count the years until retirement? In Chapter 1 we looked at the Stress Equation and saw how something apparently trivial can be the last straw and can trigger a very severe reaction to stress.

The Stress Equation:

$$S = \frac{s}{p + sup} \qquad Stress = \frac{stressor}{perception + support}$$

Let's use the example of a teacher realising that his students are writing unfair comments about him on the Internet. The 'Coping Triangle' below shows how he might feel, think and act.

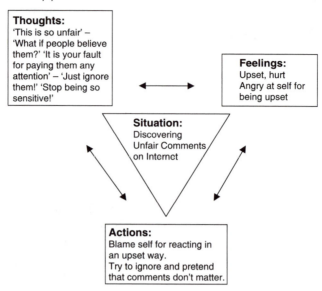

What is happening? We can see that the teacher is not allowing himself to feel angry with his students. He blames himself for 'being so sensitive' and does his best to ignore and pretend. Yes, that approach will probably work for a while, but most of us could not but be upset at such an unjust attack by students, and possibly their parents. I hope that having read this book you are very clear that the teacher's feelings of hurt and upset make sense given that he is human. His anger towards himself might surprise us until we realise that it is a consequence of how harsh and critical he is towards himself for feeling upset! His thoughts are clearly unhelpful, as are his actions of blaming himself, ignoring and pretending. So what can he do? As we have seen, it is action that makes the difference. Sometimes ignoring does work, but in this instance I am not sure. Certainly parents and students need a system to process their feelings of dissatisfaction about a teacher. I don't think anyone would dispute that. Use of the Internet, however, makes me think of students scribbling their comments on the back of toilet doors – how do schools generally deal with that? They clean them and are very clear that such behaviour is outside the school's code of discipline. Just think of the uproar there would be if teachers decided to respond to this cruel treatment by writing comments about their students on the Internet!

What might a strong 'Coping Sentence' be in this situation?

'I feel hurt and attacked because horrible things have been written about me by some students *but I choose to keep a wider perspective on my ability to teach*.'

'I am angry with myself because I think I am too sensitive to take those comments seriously but *I am human too!*'

Teachers are human. The inevitable consequence of too much stress relative to the internal and external supports available is a human being who 'suffers' from stress. This may take the form of anger, anxiety, depression or indeed serious physical illnesses such as cancer. As we know, many teachers then judge themselves harshly for their 'inability' to cope with stress, with the result of exacerbating the situation. It is time for us to recognise and appreciate teachers as human beings who are expected to do super-human jobs.

The tsunami in Asia in December 2004 tragically caused deaths of thousands of people and ruined the lives of many, many more. In the midst of the horror one wonderful story emerged about how Tilly Smith, a ten-year-old British schoolgirl, had been taught about tsunamis a few weeks earlier in a geography class by her teacher, Andrew Kearney. James Owen, writing in the *National Geographic News* (Owen, 2005), describes how Tilly sensed that there was something wrong in the vital few minutes before the tsunami struck and as a result saved the lives of her family as well as other people on the beach who were alerted by her distress. Owen quotes Kearney as saying 'People underrate teaching and teachers and they feel it's important to show we can make a difference' (Owen, 2005: 3).

Teachers do make a difference. Most of the time we will never know just how much of a difference. External recognition is lovely when we get it, but we need to continually recognise ourselves for the great work we do. Teaching can be stressful and we have a duty of care to ourselves as well as to our students to cope with it as well as we can.

The 'Coping Triangle' encourages us to:

1 Identify and acknowledge feelings and see if they make sense.
2 Identify thoughts and determine if they are helpful or unhelpful.
3 Identify current actions and determine if they are helpful or unhelpful.
4 Devise a strong 'Coping Sentence': 'I feel ____ because ____ but ____.'
5 Create ways to remind us of our 'Coping Sentence' such as writing it on notes to carry in pockets, bags, books, etc.
6 Generate a list of more helpful actions and work at implementing them.

Some 'helpful actions' might include:

1 Obtaining professional support from a GP, and/or therapist.
2 Developing the support structures available within your school.
3 Creating a balance between work, rest and play.
4 Doing at least one 'fun thing' each day.
5 Acknowledging yourself for effort as well as achievement.
6 Reminding yourself of what you love about teaching.

I would like to conclude by suggesting a 'Coping Sentence' for daily use that focuses you on (a) acknowledging how you feel, (b) linking it to something that makes sense and then (c) moving to consider exactly how you can relieve that stress:

I feel ＿＿＿ because ＿＿＿

but I love teaching and I choose to relieve my stress now!

References

Albano, A., Clarke, G., Heimberg, R. and Kendall, P.C. (1997) 'Coping with stress course', unpublished manuscript. Temple University.

American Psychiatric Association (1994) *Diagnostic and Statistical Manual of Mental Disorders* (4th edn). Washington: American Psychiatric Press.

Bandura, A. (1977) 'Self-efficacy: Toward a unifying theory of behavioural change'. *Psychological Review*, 84, 191–215.

Bandura, A. (1997) *Self-efficacy. The Exercise of Control*. New York: W.H. Freeman and Co.

Barrett, P.M., Dadds, M.R. and Rapee, R.M. (1996) 'Family treatment of childhood anxiety: A controlled trial'. *Journal of Consulting and Clinical Psychology*, 64, 333–342.

Barrett, P.M., Duffy, A.L., Dadds, M.R. and Rapee, R.M. (2001) 'Cognitive-behavioural treatment of anxiety disorders in children: Long-term (6-year) follow-up'. *Journal of Consulting and Clinical Psychology*, 69, 135–141.

Bates, A. (1993) 'Cognitive behavioural therapy', in E. Boyne (ed.) *Psychotherapy in Ireland*. Dublin: Columba Press.

Bates, T. (1999) *Depression: The Common Sense Approach*. Dublin: Newleaf.

Beck, A.T. (1963) 'Thinking and depression; 1. Idiosyncratic content and cognitive distortions'. *Archives of General Psychiatry*, 9, 324–333.

Beck, A.T. (1967) *Depression: Clinical, Experimental and Theoretical Aspects*. New York: Harper & Row.

Beck, A.T. (1978) *Depression Inventory*. Philadelphia: Center for Cognitive Therapy.

Beck, A.T. and Emery, G. (1985) *Anxiety Disorders and Phobias: A Cognitive Perspective*. USA: Basic Books.

Beck, A.T., Rush, A.J., Shaw, B. and Emery, G. (1979) *Cognitive Therapy of Depression*. New York: Guilford.

Berry, C.R. (1988) *When Helping You is Hurting Me. Escaping the Messiah Trap*. New York: HarperCollins.

Berry, C.R. (1991) *How to Escape the Messiah Trap. A Workbook for When Helping You is Hurting Me*. New York: HarperCollins.

Blonna, R. (1996) *Coping with Stress in a Changing World*. USA: Mosby-Year Book.

Bourne, E. (2000) *The Anxiety and Phobia Workbook* (3rd edn). USA: New Harbinger Publications.

Boyzone (1998) 'No matter what', on *Where we Belong* (compact disc). Dublin: Polygram Ireland.

Braet, C. (1999) 'Treatment of obese children: A new rationale'. *Clinical Child Psychiatry*, 4 (4), 579–591.

Burns, D. (1980) *Feeling Good: The New Mood Therapy*. New York: Avon.

Burns, D. (1989) *The Feeling Good Handbook*. USA: Plume.

Burns, D. (1999) *Ten Days to Great Self-Esteem*. London: Vermilion.

Butler, G. (1999) *Overcoming Social Anxiety: A Self-help Guide Using Cognitive Behavioural Techniques*. UK: Constable & Robinson.

Butler, G. and Hope, T. (1998) *Manage your Mind*. Oxford: Oxford University Press.

Caplan, G. (1964) *Principles of Preventive Psychiatry*. London: Tavistock Publications Ltd.

Carr, A. (1999) *The Handbook of Child and Adolescent Clinical Psychology. A Contextual Approach*. London: Routledge.

Chödrön, P. (2001) *The Places that Scare you. A Guide to Fearlessness in Difficult Times*. Boston: Shambhala Publications.

Christenson, S.L. and Brooke Carroll, E. (1999) 'Strengthening the family–school partnership through "Check and Connect"', in E. Frydenberg (ed.) *Learning to Cope: Developing as a Person in Complex Societies*. New York: Oxford University Press.

Clarke, G.N., Hawkins, W., Murphy, M., Sheeber, L., Lewinsohn, P.M. and Seeley, J.R. (1995) 'Targeted prevention of unipolar depressive disorder in an at-risk sample of high-school adolescents: a randomised trial of a group cognitive intervention'. *Journal of the American Academy of Child and Adolescent Psychiatry*, 34, 312–321.

Clarke, G.N., Lewinsohn, P.M. and Hops, H. (1990) *Adolescent Coping with Depression Course*. Oregon: Castalia Press.

Coley, J. and Dwivedi, K.N. (2004) 'Life skills education through schools', in K.N. Dwivedi and P. Brinley Harper (eds) *Promoting the Emotional Well-being of Children and Adolescents and Preventing their Mental Ill Health*. UK: Jessica Kingsley Publishers.

Coolahan, J. (2000) 'Teacher education in Ireland and Western Europe: A comparative analysis', in S. Drudy and E. Oldham (eds) *Educating the Educators. Proceedings of a Conference on Teacher Education*. Ireland: Educational Studies Association of Ireland.

Corey, G. (1996) *Theory and Practice of Counselling and Psychotherapy* (5th edn). USA: Brooks Cole.

Cuijpers, P. (1998) 'A psychoeducational approach to treatment of depression: A meta-analysis of Lewinsohn's "Coping with Depression" Course'. *Behaviour Therapy*, 29, 521–533.

Diekstra, R.F.W., Kienhorst, C.W.M. and de Wilde, E.J. (1995) 'Suicide and suicidal behaviour among adolescents', in M. Rutter and D. Smith (eds) *Psychosocial Disorders in Young People*. London: John Wiley.

Divinyi, J.E. (1995) 'Storytelling: An enjoyable and effective therapeutic tool'. *Contemporary Family Therapy*, 7 (1), 27–37.

Doka, K.J. (2000) *Living with Grief. Children, Adolescents and Loss*. USA: Brunner-Mazel.

Dornbusch, S.M., Laird, J. and Crosnoe, R. (1999) 'Parental and school resources that assist adolescents in coping with negative peer influences', in E. Frydenberg (ed.) *Learning to Cope: Developing as a Person in Complex Societies*. New York: Oxford University Press.

Dowrick, C., Dunn, G., Ayuso-Mateos, J.L., Dalgard, O.S., Page, H., Lehtinen, V., Wilkinson, C., Vazquez-Barquero, J.L., Wilkinson, G. and The ODIN Group (2000) 'Problem-solving treatment and group psycho-education for depression: Multicentre randomised controlled trial'. *British Medical Journal*, 321, 1450–1454.

Dryden (2001) *Reason to Change: A Rational Emotive Behaviour Therapy (REBT) Workbook*. UK: Brunner Routledge.

Dweck, C. (1998) 'The development of early self-conceptions: their relevance to motivational processes', in J. Heckhausen and C.S. Dweck (eds) *Motivation and Self-regulation Across the Life-span*. New York: Cambridge University Press.

Dwivedi, K.N. and Brinley Harper, P. (eds) (2004) *Promoting the Emotional Well-being of Children and Adolescents and Preventing Their Mental Ill Health*. UK: Jessica Kingsley Publishers.

Dwivedi, K.N. and Varma, V.P. (1997) *Depression in Children and Adolescents*. London: Whurr Publishers.

Eisenberg, N. (1998) 'Introduction', in W. Damon and N. Eisenberg (eds) *Handbook of Child Psychology* (5th edn), Vol. 3. New York: John Wiley and Sons.

Ellis, A. (1962) *Reason and Emotion in Psychotherapy*. New York: Lyle Stuart.

Ellis, A. (1993) 'Reflections on rational emotive therapy'. *Journal of Consulting and Clinical Psychology*, 61 (2), 199–201.

Ellis, A. and Harper, R. (1975) *A New Guide to Rational Living*. North Hollywood: Wilshire Books.

Fennell, M. (1999) *Overcoming Low Self-esteem: Self-help Guide Using Cognitive Behavioural Techniques*. UK: Constable & Robinson.

Fielding, H. (2001) *Bridget Jones's Diary: A Novel*. UK: Picador.

Fielding, H. (2004) *Bridget Jones: The Return to Reason*. UK: Picador.

Friedberg, R.B. (1996) 'Cognitive-behavioural games and workbooks: Tips for school counsellors'. *Elementary School Guidance and Counselling*, 31, 11–20.

Friedman, M. and Rosenman, R. (1974) *Type A Behaviour and Your Heart*. USA: Fawcett.

Frydenberg, E. (1997) *Adolescent Coping. Theoretical and Research Perspectives*. London: Routledge.

Frydenberg, E. (ed.) (1999) *Learning to Cope: Developing as a Person in Complex Societies*. New York: Oxford University Press.

Ghuman, H.S. and Sarles, R.M. (1998) *Handbook of Child and Adolescent Outpatient, Day Treatment and Community Psychiatry*. New York: Taylor & Francis.

Gilbert, P. (2000) *Overcoming Depression: A Self-help Guide Using Cognitive Behavioural Techniques*. UK: Constable & Robinson.

Gilbert, P. (ed.) (2005) *Compassion: Conceptualisations Research and Use in Psychotherapy*. London: Brunner-Routledge.

Gootman, M.E. (1994) *When a Friend Dies*. USA: Free Spirit Publishing.

Graham, P. (ed.) (1998) *Cognitive-behaviour Therapy for Children and Families*. Cambridge: Cambridge University Press.

Gray, G. (1992) *Men are from Mars, Women are from Venus*. London: Thorsons.

Greenberger, D. and Padesky, C. (1995) *Mind over Mood*. USA: Guilford Press.

Hammer, A.L. and Marting (1987) *Coping Resources Inventory*. California: Consulting Psychologists Press.

Hart, P.M., Wearing, A.J. and Conn, M. (1995) 'Conventional wisdom is a poor predictor of the relationship between discipline policy, student misbehaviour and teacher stress'. *British Journal of Educational Psychology*, 65 (1), 27–48.

Hayes, C. (1999) 'A simple approach to coping with stress'. *Journal of the Institute of Guidance Counsellors*, 23, 70–72.

Hayes, C. (2000) 'Hope for the "helping messiah"'. *Journal of the Institute of Guidance Counsellors*, 24, 3–10.

Hayes, C. (2001a) 'Helping adolescents cope: A psychoeducational approach', unpublished doctoral dissertation. Dublin City University.

Hayes, C. (2001b) 'A psychoeducational approach to helping adolescents cope'. *Irish Educational Studies*, 20, 97–106.

Hayes, C. (2004) 'Prevention of depression and anxiety in children and adolescents', in K.N. Dwivedi and P.B. Harper (eds) *Handbook for Promoting Emotional Well-being of Children and Adolescents and Preventing their Mental Ill Health. A Handbook*. UK: Jessica Kingsley Publishers.

Hayes, C. and Morgan, M. (2005) 'A psychoeducational approach to preventing depression and anxiety'. *Journal of Youth and Adolescence*, 34 (2), 111–121.

Head, J. (1997) *Working with Adolescents. Constructing Identity*. London: Falmer Press.

Heegaard, M. (1991) *When Someone Very Special Dies. Children can Learn to Cope with Grief*. USA: Woodland Press.

Holmes, H.T. and Rahe, H.R. (1967) 'The social readjustment rating scale'. *Journal of Psychosomatic Research*, 11, 213.

Ireland (1996) *Putting Children First: A Discussion Document on Mandatory Reporting of Child Abuse*. Dublin: Govt. Publications Office.

Ireland (1999) *Children First: National Guidelines for the Protection and Welfare of Children*. Dublin: Govt. Publications Office.

Ireland (2001) *Child Protection – Guidelines and Procedures*. Dublin: Govt. Publications Office.

Ireland (2004) *Child Protection Guidelines for Post-Primary Schools*. Dublin: Govt. Publications Office.

James, J.E. and Gregg, M.E. (2004a) 'Hemodynamic effects of dietary caffeine, sleep restriction and laboratory stress'. *Psychophysiology*, 41, 914–923.

James, J.E. and Gregg, M.E. (2004b) 'Effects of dietary caffeine on mood when rested and sleep restricted'. *Human Psychopharmalogical Clinical Experiments*, 19, 1–9.

Jarvis, M. (2002) 'Teacher stress: A critical review of recent findings and suggestions for future research directions'. *Stress News*, 14, 1.

Jaycock, L.H., Reivich, K.J., Gillham, J. and Seligman, M.E. (1994) 'Prevention of depressive symptoms in school children'. *Behaviour Research and Theory*, 32, 801–816.

Jeffers, S. (1989) *Feel the Fear and Do it Anyway*. London: Century.

Kendall, P.C. (1992) *Coping Cat Workbook*. Ardmore, PA: Workbook Publishing.

Kendall, P.C. (1993) 'Cognitive-behavioural therapies with young children: Guiding theory, current status, and emerging developments'. *Journal of Consulting and Clinical Psychology*, 61, 235–247.

Kendall, P.C. (1994) 'Treating anxiety disorders in children: Results of a randomised clinical trial'. *Journal of Consulting and Clinical Psychology*, 62, 100–110.

Kendall, P.C. (1998) 'Directing misperceptions: Researching the issues facing manual-based treatments'. *American Psychological Association*, 5, 396–399.

Kendall, P.C. and Flannery-Schroeder, E.C. (1998) 'Methodological issues in treatment research for anxiety disorders in youth'. *Journal of Abnormal Child Psychology*, 26, 27–39.

Kendall, P.C. and Southam-Gerow, M. (1996) 'Long-term follow-up of a cognitive-behavioural therapy for anxiety-disordered youth'. *Journal of Consulting and Clinical Psychology*, 64, 724–730.

Kendall, P.C., Chu, B., Gifford, A., Hayes, C. and Nauta, M. (1998) 'Breathing life into a manual: Flexibility and variety with manual-based treatments'. *Cognitive and Behavioural Practice*, 5, 177–198.

Kendall, P.C., Panichelli-Mindel, S.M., Sugarman, A. and Callahan, S.A. (1997) 'Exposure to child anxiety: Theory, research and practice'. *Clinical Psychology: Science and Practice*, 4, 29–39.

Kennerley, H. (1997) *Overcoming Anxiety: A Self-help Guide to Using Cognitive Behavioural Techniques*. UK: Constable & Robinson.

Kobassa, S. (1979) 'Stressful life events, personality and health: An inquiry into hardiness'. *Journal of Personality and Social Psychology*, 37 (1), 1–11.

Kovacs, M. (1992) *Children's Depression Inventory*. New York: Multi-Health Systems.

Kubler-Ross, E. (1983) *On Children and Death*. USA: Collier Books.

Kyriacou, C. (2001) 'Teacher stress: Directions for future research', *Educational Review*, 53 (1), 27–35.

Labellarte, M.J., Ginsburg, G.S., Walkup, J.T. and Riddle, M.A. (1999) 'The treatment of anxiety disorders in children and adolescents'. *Biological Psychiatry*, 46, 1567–1578.

Lazarus, R.S. (1966) *Psychological Stress and the Coping Process*. New York: McGraw-Hill.

Lazarus, R.S. (1991) *Emotion and Adaptation*. New York: Oxford University Press.

Lazarus, R.S. and Folkman, S. (1985) *Stress Appraisal and Coping*. New York: Springer.

Leaman, O. (1995) *Death and Loss. Compassionate Approaches in the Classroom*. London: Cassell.

Lewinsohn, P.M. and Clarke, G.N. (1999) 'Psychosocial treatments for adolescent depression'. *Clinical Psychology Review*, 19, 329–342.

Lewinsohn, P.M., Antonuccio, D.O., Steinmetz, J. and Teri, L. (1984) *The Coping with Depression Course: A Psychoeducational Intervention for Unipolar Depression*. Eugene, OR: Castalia.

Lewinsohn, P.M., Clarke, G.N., Hops, H. and Andrews, J. (1990) 'Cognitive-behavioural treatment of depressed adolescents'. *Behaviour Therapy*, 21, 385–401.

Lewinsohn, P.M., Clarke, G.N., Rohde, P., Hops, H. and Seeley, J.R. (1996) 'A course in coping: A cognitive-behavioural approach to the treatment of adolescent depression', in E.D. Hibbs and P. Jensen (eds) *Psychosocial Treatments for Child and Adolescent Disorders: Empirically Based Strategies for Clinical Practice*. Washington, DC: American Psychological Association.

Lewis, R. (1999) 'Teachers coping with the stress of classroom discipline'. *Social Psychology of Education*, 3, 155–171.

Lindenfield, G. (2000) *Self-esteem*. London: Thorsons.

Lindenfield, G. and Vanderburg, M. (2000) *Positive under Pressure*. London: Thorsons.

MacIntyre, D. and Carr, A. (1999) 'Helping children to the other side of silence: A study of the impact of the stay safe programme on Irish children's disclosures of sexual victimisation'. *Child Abuse and Neglect*, 23, 1327–1340.

MacIntyre, D. and Lawlor, M. (1991) *The Stay Safe Programme*. Dublin: Government Publications.

Martin, M. (1997) *Discipline in Schools*. Dublin: Government Publications.

McKay, M. and Fanning, P. (2000) *Self-Esteem: A Proven Program of Cognitive Techniques for Assessing, Improving and Maintaining Your Self-Esteem* (3rd edn). USA: Harbinger.

McNamara, S. (2000) *Stress in Young People. What's New and What can we Do?* London: Continuum.

McNamara, S. (2001) *Stress Management Programme for Secondary School Students*. London: RoutledgeFalmer.

Meichenbaum, D. (1977) *Cognitive Behavior Modification: An Integrative Approach*. New York: Plenum.

Meichenbaum, D. (1986) 'Cognitive behavior modification', in F.H. Kanfer and A.P. Goldstein (eds) *Helping People Change: A Textbook of Methods*. New York: Pergamon Press.

Messent, P. (2004) 'Ethnic minority children and families and mental health: Preventive approaches', in K.N. Dwivedi and P. Brinley Harper (eds) *Promoting the Emotional Well-being of Children and Adolescents and Preventing Their Mental Ill Health*. UK: Jessica Kingsley Publishers.

Meyer, R.J. (1996) *Stories from the Heart. Teachers and Students Researching their Literacy Lives*. New Jersey: Lawrence Erlbaum Associates.

Moore, K.A., Sugland, B.W., Blumenthal, C., Glei, D. and Snyder, N. (1995) *Adolescent Pregnancy Prevention Programs: Interventions and Evaluations*. Washington, DC: Child Trends.

Moore, S. (1999) 'Sexuality in adolescence: A suitable case for coping?' in E. Frydenberg (ed.) *Learning to Cope: Developing as a Person in Complex Societies*. New York: Oxford University Press.

Morgan, M. (2000) *Relationships and Sexuality Education. An Evaluation and Review of Implementation*. Dublin: Government of Ireland Publications.

Morgan, M., Morrow, R., Sheehan, A.M. and Lillis, M. (1996) 'Prevention of substance misuse: Rationale and effectiveness of the programme "On My Own Two Feet"'. *Oideas: Journal of the Department of Education*, 44, 5–26.

Muldoon, O. and Cairns, E. (1999) 'Children, young people and war: Learning to cope', in E. Frydenberg (ed.) *Learning to Cope: Developing as a Person in Complex Societies*. New York: Oxford University Press.

Nauta, M.H. (2005) *Anxiety Disorders in Children and Adolescents: Assessment, Cognitive Behavioural Therapy and Predictors of Treatment Outcome*. Netherlands: Febodruk.

Nitz, K. (1999) 'Adolescent pregnancy prevention. A review of interventions and programs'. *Clinical Psychology Review*, 19, 457–471.

O'Connor, R. and Sheehy, N.P. (2001) 'Contemporary perspectives on suicide'. *The Psychologist*, 14, 20–25.

Olweus, D. (1994) 'Annotation: Bullying at school: Basic facts and effects of a school based intervention program'. *Journal of Child Psychology and Psychiatry*, 35, 1171–1190.

Owen, J. (2005) 'Tsunami family saved by schoolgirl's geography lesson'. Online. Available HTTP: http://news.nationalgeographic.com/news/2005/01/0118_050118_tsunami_geography_lesson.html (accessed 29 May 2005).

Piaget, J. (1958) *The Growth of Logical Thinking from Childhood to Adolescence*. New York: Basic Books.

Piaget, J. (1983) 'Piaget's theory', in P.H. Mussen (ed.) *Handbook of Child Psychology: Vol. 1. History, Theory and Methods*. New York: Wiley.

Pithers, R.T. and Soden, R. (1998) 'Scottish and Australian teacher stress and strain: A comparative study'. *British Journal of Educational Psychology*, 68, 269–279.

Porteous, M.A. (1997) *Porteous Problem Checklist*. Cork, Ireland: Psychometrica International Ltd.

Reynolds, W.M. and Coates, K.I. (1986) 'A comparison of cognitive-behavioural therapy and relaxation training for the treatment of depression in adolescents'. *Journal of Consulting and Clinical Psychology*, 54, 653–660.

Rice, K.G. and Meyer, A.L. (1994) 'Preventing depression among young adolescents: Preliminary process results of a psycho-educational intervention program'. *Journal of Counselling and Development*, 73, 145–152.

Rogers, C. (1951) *Client-Centered Therapy*. Boston: Houghton Mifflin.

Rogers, C. (1980) *A Way of Being*. Boston: Houghton Mifflin.

Rogers, C. (1986) 'Client-centered therapy', in I.L. Kutash and A. Wolf (eds) *Psychotherapist's Casebook*. San Francisco: Jossey-Bass.

Rollin, S.A., Anderson, C.W. and Buncher, R.M. (1999) 'Coping in children and adolescents: A prevention model for helping kids avoid or reduce at-risk behaviour', in E. Frydenberg (ed.) *Learning to Cope: Developing as a Person in Complex Societies*. New York: Oxford University Press.

Rosenman, R. and Chesney, M.A. (1985) 'Type A behaviour and coronary disease', in C.D. Spielberger and I.G. Sarason (eds) *Stress and Anxiety*. Vol. 9. Washington, DC: Hemisphere.

Rutter, M. (1985) 'Resilience in the face of adversity: Protective factors and resistance to psychiatric disorders', *British Journal of Psychiatry*, 147, 589–611.

Rutter, M. (1990) 'Psychosocial resilience and protective mechanisms', in J. Rolf, A.S. Masten, D. Cicchetti, K.H. Nuechterlein and S. Weintraub (eds) *Risk and Protective Factors in the Development of Psychopathology*. New York: Cambridge University Press.

Seligman, M. (1992) *Learned Optimism*. NSW, Australia: Random House.

Seligman, M. (1995) *The Optimistic Child*. NSW, Australia: Random House.

Seligman, M.P., Schulman, P., DeRubeis, R.J. and Hollon, S.D. (1999) 'The prevention of depression and anxiety'. *Prevention and Treatment*, 2, Article 8. Online. Available HTTP: http://www.journals.apa.org/prevention/volume2/pre0020008a.html (accessed 22 May 2005).

Selye, H. (1956) *The Stress of Life*. New York: McGraw-Hill.

Selye, H. (1974) *Stress Without Distress*. USA: Lipincott.

Smilansky, S. (1987) *On Death: Helping Children Understand and Cope*. New York: Peter Lang Publishing.

Stallard, P. (2002) *Think Good – Feel Good: A Cognitive Behaviour Therapy Workbook for Children and Young People*. Chichester: Wiley.

Stark, K.D. and Kendall, P.C. (1996) *Treating Depressed Children: Therapist Manual for 'Action'*. PA: Workbook Publishing.

Stark, K.D. and Smith, A. (1995) 'Cognitive and behavioural treatment of childhood depression', in H.P.J. Van Bilsen (ed.) *Behavioural Approaches for Children and Adolescents*. New York: Plenum Press.

Stark, K.D., Rouse, L.W. and Livingston, R. (1991) 'Treatment of depression during childhood and adolescence: Cognitive-behavioural procedures for the individual and family', in P.C. Kendall (ed.) *Child and Adolescent Therapy: Cognitive-behavioural Procedures*. New York: Guilford Press.

Stewart, A. (2004) 'Prevention of eating disorders', in K.N. Dwivedi and P.B. Harper (eds) *Handbook for Promoting Emotional Well-being of Children and Adolescents and Preventing Their Mental Ill Health. A Handbook*. UK: Jessica Kingsley Publishers.

Stone, S., Patton, B. and Heen, S. (1999) *Difficult Conversations: How to Discuss what Matters Most*. UK: Penguin.

Tatelbaum, J. (1997) *The Courage to Grieve*. London: Vermilion.

Thich Nhat Hanh (1991) *Peace is Every Step*. London: Rider.

Thich Nhat Hanh (1991) *The Miracle of Mindfulness. A Manual on Meditation*. London: Rider.

Tinzmann, M.D. and Hikson, J. (1992) *What Does Research Say about Prevention?* New York: Oak Brook.

Travers, C. and Cooper, C. (1997) 'Stress in teaching', in D. Shorrocks-Taylor (ed.). *Directions in Educational Psychology*. London: Whurr.

Waddell, C., Lipman, E. and Offord, D. (1999) 'Conduct disorder: Practice parameters for assessment, treatment and prevention'. *Canadian Journal of Psychiatry*, 44, Suppl 2, 35S–40S.

Waldsax, A. (2004) 'Parenting', in K.N. Dwivedi and P.B. Brinley Harper (eds) *Promoting the Emotional Well-being of Children and Adolescents and Preventing Their Mental Ill Health*. UK: Jessica Kingsley Publishers.

Wass, H. and Corr, A. (1982) *Helping Children Cope with Death: Guidelines and Resources.* Washington: Hemisphere Publishing Corporation.

Weishaar, M.E. (1993) *Aaron T. Beck.* London: Sage.

Weissberg, R.P. and Greenberg, M.T. (1998) 'School and community competence-enhancement and prevention programs', in W. Damon, I.E. Sigel and A. Renningar (eds) *Handbook of Child Psychology* (5th edn), Vol. 3. New York: John Wiley and Sons.

Weist, M.D. (1998) 'Mental health services in schools: Expanding opportunities', in H.S. Ghuman and R.M. Sarles (eds) *Handbook of Child and Adolescent Outpatient, Day Treatment and Community Psychiatry.* New York: Taylor & Francis.

Weist, M.D. and Danforth, J.S. (1998) 'Cognitive-behavioural therapy with children and adolescents', in H.S. Ghuman and R.M. Sarles (eds) *Handbook of Child and Adolescent Outpatient, Day Treatment and Community Psychiatry.* New York: Taylor & Francis.

Weisz, J.R., Weiss, B., Han, S.S., Granger, D.A. and Morton, T. (1995) 'Effects of psychotherapy with children and adolescents revisited: A meta-analysis of treatment outcome studies'. *Psychological Bulletin,* 117, 450–468.

Williams, J.R. (1995) 'Using story as metaphor, legacy and therapy'. *Contemporary Family Therapy,* 7 (1), 9–16.

World Health Organisation (1997) *Life Skills Education in Schools.* Geneva: Division of Mental Health and Prevention of Substance Abuse.